JAMESTOWN EDUCATION

Reading Fluency

Reader's Record

Level J

Camille L. Z. Blachowicz, Ph.D.

JAMESTOWN EDUCATION

Reading Fluency

Reader's Record

Level
J

Camille L. Z. Blachowicz, Ph.D.

New York, New York   Columbus, Ohio   Chicago, Illinois   Peoria, Illinois   Woodland Hills, California

JAMESTOWN EDUCATION

Glencoe

The *McGraw-Hill* Companies

Send all inquiries to:
Glencoe/McGraw-Hill
8787 Orion Place
Columbus, OH 43240-4027

ISBN: 0-07-861714-6
Printed in the United States of America.
2 3 4 5 6 7 8 9 10 021 10 09 08 07 06

Contents

The passages in this book are taken from the following sources.

How to Use These Books

The Reading Fluency *Reader* contains 72 reading passages. The accompanying *Reader's Record* contains two copies of each of these passages and includes a place for marking *miscues*. You and your partner will take turns using the *Reader*. Each of you will need your own *Reader's Record*. You will also need a stopwatch or a timer.

What Are Miscues?

Miscues are errors or slips that all readers make. These include the following:
- a mispronounced word
- a word substituted for the correct word
- an inserted word
- a skipped word

Repeating a word or correcting oneself immediately is not counted as a miscue.

What Procedure Do I Follow?

1. Work with a partner. One partner is the reader; the other partner is the recorder.

2. Suppose that you are the first to read aloud. Read a selection from the *Reader* as your partner marks any miscues you make on the corresponding page in your *Reader's Record*. The recorder's job is to listen carefully and make a tick mark above each place in the text where a miscue occurs, and to make a slash mark indicating where you stop reading after "Time!" is called.

3. The recorder says when to start and calls "Time!" after a minute.

4. After the reading, the recorder:
- counts the number of words read, using the number guides at the right-hand side of the passage, and records the Total Words Read
- writes the total number of miscues for each line in the far right-hand column labeled Miscues. Totals and records the miscues on the Total Errors line
- subtracts Total Errors from Total Words Read to find the Correct Words Per Minute (WPM) and records that score on the Correct WPM line

5. You review the *Reader's Record*, noting your miscues. Discuss with your partner the characteristics of good reading you have displayed. Then rate your own performance and mark the scale at the bottom of the page.

6. Change roles with your partner and repeat the procedure.

7. You and your partner then begin a second round of reading the same passage. When it is your turn to read, try to improve in pace, expression, and accuracy over the first reading.

8. After completing two readings, record your Correct WPM scores in the back of your *Reader's Record*. Follow the directions on the graph.

from "The Laughing Man"

Fiction by J. D. Salinger

First Reading

Listen as the narrator launches into another installment of the adventure serial "The Laughing Man."

	Words Read	Miscues

A flux of circumstances delivered the Laughing Man's best — 9 ———

friend, his timber wolf, Black Wing, into a physical and — 19 ———

intellectual trap set by the Dufarges. The Dufarges, aware of the — 30 ———

Laughing Man's high sense of loyalty, offered him Black Wing's — 40 ———

freedom in exchange for his own. In the best faith in the world, — 53 ———

the Laughing Man agreed to these terms. (Some of the minor — 64 ———

mechanics of his genius were often subject to mysterious little — 74 ———

breakdowns.) It was arranged for the Laughing Man to meet the — 85 ———

Dufarges at midnight in a designated section of the dense forest — 96 ———

surrounding Paris, and there, by moonlight, Black Wing would — 105 ———

be set free. However, the Dufarges had no intention of liberating — 116 ———

Black Wing, whom they feared and loathed. On the night of — 127 ———

the transaction, they leashed a stand-in timber wolf for Black — 137 ———

Wing, first dyeing its left hind foot snow white, to look like — 149 ———

Black Wing's. — 151 ———

But there were two things the Dufarges hadn't counted on: — 161 ———

the Laughing Man's sentimentality and his command of the — 170 ———

timber-wolf language. As soon as he had allowed Dufarge's — 179 ———

daughter to tie him with barbed wire to a tree, the Laughing Man — 192 ———

felt called upon to raise his beautiful, melodious voice in a few — 204 ———

words of farewell to his supposed old friend. — 212 ———

Needs Work   1 2 3 4 5   Excellent
Paid attention to punctuation

Needs Work   1 2 3 4 5   Excellent
Sounded good

Total Words Read _____

Total Errors − _____

Correct WPM _____

from "The Laughing Man"

by J. D. Salinger

Listen as the narrator launches into another installment of the
adventure serial "The Laughing Man."

	Second Reading
Words Read	**Miscues**

A flux of circumstances delivered the Laughing Man's best
friend, his timber wolf, Black Wing, into a physical and
intellectual trap set by the Dufarges. The Dufarges, aware of the
Laughing Man's high sense of loyalty, offered him Black Wing's
freedom in exchange for his own. In the best faith in the world,
the Laughing Man agreed to these terms. (Some of the minor
mechanics of his genius were often subject to mysterious little
breakdowns.) It was arranged for the Laughing Man to meet the
Dufarges at midnight in a designated section of the dense forest
surrounding Paris, and there, by moonlight, Black Wing would
be set free. However, the Dufarges had no intention of liberating
Black Wing, whom they feared and loathed. On the night of
the transaction, they leashed a stand-in timber wolf for Black
Wing, first dyeing its left hind foot snow white, to look like
Black Wing's.

But there were two things the Dufarges hadn't counted on:
the Laughing Man's sentimentality and his command of the
timber-wolf language. As soon as he had allowed Dufarge's
daughter to tie him with barbed wire to a tree, the Laughing Man
felt called upon to raise his beautiful, melodious voice in a few
words of farewell to his supposed old friend.

Words Read
9
19
30
40
53
64
74
85
96
105
116
127
137
149
151
161
170
179
192
204
212

Needs Work   1   2   3   4   5   Excellent
Paid attention to punctuation

Needs Work   1   2   3   4   5   Excellent
Sounded good

Total Words Read _____

Total Errors − _____

Correct WPM _____

2
Fiction

from **"Shooting Stars"**
by Denise Chávez

Read about the favorite imaginative game of two young girls
during their summer visit with relatives.

First Reading

	Words Read	Miscues
[Texas] was a place removed from normal experience, the	9	_____
farthest spot away from my reality. As a part of that unvoiced	21	_____
obedience to parental rule, my sister and I spent a portion of each	34	_____
summer with my mother's Texas relatives.	40	_____
One of our favorite pastimes was to sell wildflowers in a	51	_____
makeshift shop constructed by sticking clumps of stray flowers in	61	_____
my aunt's stone wall, with its cinderblock slots. We picked the	72	_____
flowers in a vacant lot sectioned off by a chain link fence that	85	_____
spiraled downward into an uncultivated field of wildflowers.	93	_____
Occasionally, the grayed and moving form of an old man	103	_____
materialized, alongside that of several angry dogs. Never was our	113	_____
flower industry totally shut down. The summer days passed this	123	_____
way, one upon another, in the ritual of the flower picking. No one	136	_____
knew of this flower industry, no one ever bought these flowers,	147	_____
but it mattered little to my sister and me. Each day we would set	161	_____
out our display, pricing and haggling between ourselves, then	170	_____
sitting down to wait for customers. It did not matter that our	182	_____
shop lay at the end of a dead-end street, or that the summer heat	196	_____
wilted customer and flower alike.	201	_____

Needs Work   1   2   3   4   5   Excellent
Paid attention to punctuation

Needs Work   1   2   3   4   5   Excellent
Sounded good

Total Words Read _____

Total Errors − _____

Correct WPM _____

from "Shooting Stars"

by Denise Chávez

Read about the favorite imaginative game of two young girls during their summer visit with relatives.

	Words Read	Miscues
[Texas] was a place removed from normal experience, the	9	_____
farthest spot away from my reality. As a part of that unvoiced	21	_____
obedience to parental rule, my sister and I spent a portion of each	34	_____
summer with my mother's Texas relatives.	40	_____
One of our favorite pastimes was to sell wildflowers in a	51	_____
makeshift shop constructed by sticking clumps of stray flowers in	61	_____
my aunt's stone wall, with its cinderblock slots. We picked the	72	_____
flowers in a vacant lot sectioned off by a chain link fence that	85	_____
spiraled downward into an uncultivated field of wildflowers.	93	_____
Occasionally, the grayed and moving form of an old man	103	_____
materialized, alongside that of several angry dogs. Never was our	113	_____
flower industry totally shut down. The summer days passed this	123	_____
way, one upon another, in the ritual of the flower picking. No one	136	_____
knew of this flower industry, no one ever bought these flowers,	147	_____
but it mattered little to my sister and me. Each day we would set	161	_____
out our display, pricing and haggling between ourselves, then	170	_____
sitting down to wait for customers. It did not matter that our	182	_____
shop lay at the end of a dead-end street, or that the summer heat	196	_____
wilted customer and flower alike.	201	_____

Needs Work   1   2   3   4   5   Excellent
Paid attention to punctuation

Needs Work   1   2   3   4   5   Excellent
Sounded good

Total Words Read _____

Total Errors − _____

Correct WPM _____

3

Nonfiction

from **"Sandra Day O'Connor"**
by Andrea Gabor

Read how the grandmother of the Supreme Court justice showed
her independent spirit.

First Reading

	Words Read	Miscues

Mamie Scott Wilkey, who cared enormously about financial | 8 | _____

security and living comfortably, would never forgive her husband | 17 | _____

for dying at the moment when he had just lost "a bundle of | 30 | _____

money," leaving her without any assets. | 36 | _____

    For Sandra, just seven years old at the time, life with Mamie | 48 | _____

Wilkey after her grandfather's death turned out to be a far more | 60 | _____

unorthodox and unsettled existence than her parents had | 68 | _____

planned. After W.W. died, Harry Day bought his mother-in-law a | 78 | _____

house in a quiet neighborhood near Sandra's school. But | 87 | _____

Grandma Wilkey had other ideas. She sold the new house to buy | 99 | _____

one that was much larger on a busier street in a less affluent | 112 | _____

neighborhood near the railroad station. Soon Mamie was taking | 121 | _____

in boarders, renting rooms for the night to engineers and | 131 | _____

brakemen who passed through El Paso on the railroad, an | 141 | _____

arrangement of which the Days heartily disapproved. Sandra grew | 150 | _____

up amid a steady stream of strangers. Even when business was | 161 | _____

relatively slow, it was never quiet in Grandma's house. Mamie | 171 | _____

Wilkey was a "nonstop talker," and Sandra would do her | 181 | _____

homework with the steady hum of Grandma's chatter in the | 191 | _____

background. "I always said that the reason I became a judge was | 203 | _____

that I learned as a child how to just listen and still get my work | 218 | _____

done," O'Connor would say years later. | 224 | _____

Needs Work   1 2 3 4 5   Excellent
     Paid attention to punctuation

Needs Work   1 2 3 4 5   Excellent
     Sounded good

Total Words Read _____

Total Errors − _____

Correct WPM _____

from "Sandra Day O'Connor"

by Andrea Gabor

Read how the grandmother of the Supreme Court justice showed her independent spirit.

Mamie Scott Wilkey, who cared enormously about financial	8
security and living comfortably, would never forgive her husband	17
for dying at the moment when he had just lost "a bundle of	30
money," leaving her without any assets.	36
For Sandra, just seven years old at the time, life with Mamie	48
Wilkey after her grandfather's death turned out to be a far more	60
unorthodox and unsettled existence than her parents had	68
planned. After W.W. died, Harry Day bought his mother-in-law a	78
house in a quiet neighborhood near Sandra's school. But	87
Grandma Wilkey had other ideas. She sold the new house to buy	99
one that was much larger on a busier street in a less affluent	112
neighborhood near the railroad station. Soon Mamie was taking	121
in boarders, renting rooms for the night to engineers and	131
brakemen who passed through El Paso on the railroad, an	141
arrangement of which the Days heartily disapproved. Sandra grew	150
up amid a steady stream of strangers. Even when business was	161
relatively slow, it was never quiet in Grandma's house. Mamie	171
Wilkey was a "nonstop talker," and Sandra would do her	181
homework with the steady hum of Grandma's chatter in the	191
background. "I always said that the reason I became a judge was	203
that I learned as a child how to just listen and still get my work	218
done," O'Connor would say years later.	224

Needs Work 1 2 3 4 5 Excellent
Paid attention to punctuation

Needs Work 1 2 3 4 5 Excellent
Sounded good

Total Words Read _____

Total Errors − _____

Correct WPM _____

4

Fiction

from *The Deerslayer*
by James Fenimore Cooper

Imagine the quiet stillness of the forest broken suddenly by voices.

First Reading

	Words Read	Miscues

Voices were heard calling to each other, in the depths of a forest,	13	_____
of which the leafy surface lay bathed in the brilliant light of a	26	_____
cloudless day in June, while the trunks of the trees rose in gloomy	39	_____
grandeur in the shades beneath. The calls were in different tones,	50	_____
evidently proceeding from two men who had lost their way, and	61	_____
were searching in different directions for their path. At length a	72	_____
shout proclaimed success, and presently a man of gigantic stature	82	_____
broke out of the tangled labyrinth of a small swamp, emerging	93	_____
into an opening that appeared to have been formed partly by the	105	_____
ravages of the wind, and partly by those of fire. This little area,	118	_____
which afforded a good view of the sky, although it was pretty well	131	_____
filled with dead trees, lay on the side of one of the high hills, or	146	_____
low mountains, into which nearly the whole surface of the	156	_____
adjacent country was broken.	160	_____

"Here is room to breathe in!" exclaimed the liberated forester, — 170

as soon as he found himself under a clear sky, shaking his huge — 183

frame like a mastiff that has just escaped from a snowbank. — 194

"Hurrah! Deerslayer; here is daylight, at last, and yonder is — 204

the lake." — 206

Needs Work 1 2 3 4 5 Excellent
Paid attention to punctuation

Needs Work 1 2 3 4 5 Excellent
Sounded good

Total Words Read _____

Total Errors − _____

Correct WPM _____

4

Fiction

from *The Deerslayer*

by James Fenimore Cooper

Imagine the quiet stillness of the forest broken suddenly by voices.

	Words Read	Miscues
Voices were heard calling to each other, in the depths of a forest,	13	_____
of which the leafy surface lay bathed in the brilliant light of a	26	_____
cloudless day in June, while the trunks of the trees rose in gloomy	39	_____
grandeur in the shades beneath. The calls were in different tones,	50	_____
evidently proceeding from two men who had lost their way, and	61	_____
were searching in different directions for their path. At length a	72	_____
shout proclaimed success, and presently a man of gigantic stature	82	_____
broke out of the tangled labyrinth of a small swamp, emerging	93	_____
into an opening that appeared to have been formed partly by the	105	_____
ravages of the wind, and partly by those of fire. This little area,	118	_____
which afforded a good view of the sky, although it was pretty well	131	_____
filled with dead trees, lay on the side of one of the high hills, or	146	_____
low mountains, into which nearly the whole surface of the	156	_____
adjacent country was broken.	160	_____
"Here is room to breathe in!" exclaimed the liberated forester,	170	_____
as soon as he found himself under a clear sky, shaking his huge	183	_____
frame like a mastiff that has just escaped from a snowbank.	194	_____
"Hurrah! Deerslayer; here is daylight, at last, and yonder is	204	_____
the lake."	206	_____

Needs Work   1 2 3 4 5   Excellent
Paid attention to punctuation

Needs Work   1 2 3 4 5   Excellent
Sounded good

Total Words Read   _____

Total Errors − _____

Correct WPM   _____

5

Fiction

from *Hullabaloo in the Guava Orchard*
by Kiran Desai

View the world from the branches of a guava tree.

First Reading

	Words Read	Miscues

Concealed in the branches of the tree he had climbed,   10 _____

Sampath felt his breathing slow and a wave of peace and   21 _____

contentment overtook him. All about him the orchard was   30 _____

spangled with the sunshine of a November afternoon, webbed   39 _____

by the reflections of the shifting foliage and filled with a liquid   51 _____

intricacy of sun and shadow. The warmth nuzzled against his   61 _____

cheek like the muzzle of an animal and, as his heartbeat grew   73 _____

quiet, he could hear the soft popping and rustling of plants being   85 _____

warmed to their different scents all about him. How beautiful it   96 _____

was here, how exactly as it should be. This orchard matched   107 _____

something he had imagined all his life: myriad green-skinned   116 _____

globes growing sweet-sour and marvelous upon a hillside with   125 _____

enough trees to fill the eye and enough fruit to scent the air. The   139 _____

leaves of these trees were just a shade darker than the fruit and   152 _____

the bark was a peeling away of tan over a milky paleness so   165 _____

delicate and so smooth that his fingers thrilled to its touch.   176 _____

And these trees were not so big, or so thick with leaves, or so   190 _____

crowded together, as to obscure the sky, which showed clean   200 _____

through the branches.   203 _____

Needs Work   1   2   3   4   5   Excellent
_____
         Paid attention to punctuation

Needs Work   1   2   3   4   5   Excellent
_____
         Sounded good

Total Words Read   _____

Total Errors   − _____

Correct WPM   _____

5

Fiction

from *Hullabaloo in the Guava Orchard*

by Kiran Desai

View the world from the branches of a guava tree.

	Words Read	Miscues
Concealed in the branches of the tree he had climbed,	10	_____
Sampath felt his breathing slow and a wave of peace and	21	_____
contentment overtook him. All about him the orchard was	30	_____
spangled with the sunshine of a November afternoon, webbed	39	_____
by the reflections of the shifting foliage and filled with a liquid	51	_____
intricacy of sun and shadow. The warmth nuzzled against his	61	_____
cheek like the muzzle of an animal and, as his heartbeat grew	73	_____
quiet, he could hear the soft popping and rustling of plants being	85	_____
warmed to their different scents all about him. How beautiful it	96	_____
was here, how exactly as it should be. This orchard matched	107	_____
something he had imagined all his life: myriad green-skinned	116	_____
globes growing sweet-sour and marvelous upon a hillside with	125	_____
enough trees to fill the eye and enough fruit to scent the air. The	139	_____
leaves of these trees were just a shade darker than the fruit and	152	_____
the bark was a peeling away of tan over a milky paleness so	165	_____
delicate and so smooth that his fingers thrilled to its touch.	176	_____
And these trees were not so big, or so thick with leaves, or so	190	_____
crowded together, as to obscure the sky, which showed clean	200	_____
through the branches.	203	_____

Needs Work   1   2   3   4   5   Excellent
_____
Paid attention to punctuation

Needs Work   1   2   3   4   5   Excellent
_____
Sounded good

Total Words Read   _____

Total Errors − _____

Correct WPM   _____

6

Nonfiction

from *Kon-Tiki:*

Across the Pacific by Raft

by Thor Heyerdahl
translated by F. H. Lyon

Learn about the author's plan to find balsa wood to build the raft
he used on his famous journey.

First Reading

	Words Read	Miscues
A little school map we found in the hotel, with green jungle,	12	_____
brown mountains, and inhabited places ringed around in red, told	22	_____
us that the jungle stretched unbroken from the Pacific right to	33	_____
the foot of the towering Andes. I had an idea. It was clearly	46	_____
impracticable now to get from the coastal area through the jungle	57	_____
to the balsa trees at Quevedo, but suppose we could get to the	70	_____
trees from the inland side, by coming straight down into the	81	_____
jungle from the bare snow mountains of the Andes range? Here	92	_____
was a possibility, the only one we saw.	100	_____
Out on the airfield we found a little cargo plane which was	112	_____
willing to take us up to Quito, the capital of this strange country,	125	_____
high up on the Andes plateau, 9,300 feet above sea level.	136	_____
Between packing cases and furniture we caught occasional	144	_____
glimpses of green jungle and shining rivers before we disappeared	154	_____
into the clouds. When we came out again, the lowlands were	165	_____
hidden under an endless sea of rolling vapor, but ahead of us dry	178	_____
mountainsides and bare cliffs rose from the sea of mist right up to	191	_____
a brilliant blue sky.	195	_____

Needs Work   1 2 3 4 5   Excellent
Paid attention to punctuation

Needs Work   1 2 3 4 5   Excellent
Sounded good

Total Words Read _____

Total Errors − _____

Correct WPM _____

from *Kon-Tiki:*

Across the Pacific by Raft

by Thor Heyerdahl
translated by F. H. Lyon

Learn about the author's plan to find balsa wood to build the raft
he used on his famous journey.

	Words Read	Miscues
A little school map we found in the hotel, with green jungle,	12	_____
brown mountains, and inhabited places ringed around in red, told	22	_____
us that the jungle stretched unbroken from the Pacific right to	33	_____
the foot of the towering Andes. I had an idea. It was clearly	46	_____
impracticable now to get from the coastal area through the jungle	57	_____
to the balsa trees at Quevedo, but suppose we could get to the	70	_____
trees from the inland side, by coming straight down into the	81	_____
jungle from the bare snow mountains of the Andes range? Here	92	_____
was a possibility, the only one we saw.	100	_____
Out on the airfield we found a little cargo plane which was	112	_____
willing to take us up to Quito, the capital of this strange country,	125	_____
high up on the Andes plateau, 9,300 feet above sea level.	136	_____
Between packing cases and furniture we caught occasional	144	_____
glimpses of green jungle and shining rivers before we disappeared	154	_____
into the clouds. When we came out again, the lowlands were	165	_____
hidden under an endless sea of rolling vapor, but ahead of us dry	178	_____
mountainsides and bare cliffs rose from the sea of mist right up to	191	_____
a brilliant blue sky.	195	_____

Needs Work 1 2 3 4 5 Excellent
Paid attention to punctuation

Needs Work 1 2 3 4 5 Excellent
Sounded good

Total Words Read _____

Total Errors − _____

Correct WPM _____

7

Nonfiction

from *Phillis Wheatley*

by Marilyn Jensen

Read about the end of the British siege of Boston in this excerpt
from a biography of a former slave.

First Reading

	Words Read	Miscues

It was actually ten days before Boston saw the last of the | 12 | _____
British, for they lingered off Nantasket Road just below Boston, | 22 | _____
giving rise to rumors that Howe might not be planning to leave | 34 | _____
the vicinity after all. But on the twenty-seventh, the strange | 44 | _____
armada sailed out to sea and headed north. Now Boston | 54 | _____
could turn its talents to repairing the damage wrought by the | 65 | _____
twenty-one month siege. | 68 | _____

It was a gigantic job, for homes had been looted, furniture | 79 | _____
smashed, stores destroyed, windows shattered, and sometimes | 86 | _____
entire walls broken out for firewood. Families who had fled | 96 | _____
at the beginning of the blockade came back to assess the damage. | 108 | _____
A few were fortunate enough to be able to move right in; others | 121 | _____
had to find temporary quarters until damages could be repaired. | 131 | _____
But while it was hard work, it was done with the buoyancy | 143 | _____
that springs from hope, for at last ships could bring in what | 155 | _____
was needed. | 157 | _____

"It's so wonderful to go to bed and know I'm not going to | 170 | _____
wake up to gunfire," Phillis said a week later as she and Master | 183 | _____
John lingered in the Lathrop parlor following Sunday dinner. | 192 | _____

"Or something burning," Mary added. | 197 | _____

"That it is," Reverend John agreed. "But we must remember | 207 | _____
this war is far from over." | 213 | _____

Needs Work   1 2 3 4 5   Excellent
Paid attention to punctuation

Needs Work   1 2 3 4 5   Excellent
Sounded good

Total Words Read _____

Total Errors − _____

Correct WPM _____

from *Phillis Wheatley*

by Marilyn Jensen

Read about the end of the British siege of Boston in this excerpt
from a biography of a former slave.

	Words Read	Miscues

It was actually ten days before Boston saw the last of the | 12 | _____

British, for they lingered off Nantasket Road just below Boston, | 22 | _____

giving rise to rumors that Howe might not be planning to leave | 34 | _____

the vicinity after all. But on the twenty-seventh, the strange | 44 | _____

armada sailed out to sea and headed north. Now Boston | 54 | _____

could turn its talents to repairing the damage wrought by the | 65 | _____

twenty-one month siege. | 68 | _____

It was a gigantic job, for homes had been looted, furniture | 79 | _____

smashed, stores destroyed, windows shattered, and sometimes | 86 | _____

entire walls broken out for firewood. Families who had fled | 96 | _____

at the beginning of the blockade came back to assess the damage. | 108 | _____

A few were fortunate enough to be able to move right in; others | 121 | _____

had to find temporary quarters until damages could be repaired. | 131 | _____

But while it was hard work, it was done with the buoyancy | 143 | _____

that springs from hope, for at last ships could bring in what | 155 | _____

was needed. | 157 | _____

"It's so wonderful to go to bed and know I'm not going to | 170 | _____

wake up to gunfire," Phillis said a week later as she and Master | 183 | _____

John lingered in the Lathrop parlor following Sunday dinner. | 192 | _____

"Or something burning," Mary added. | 197 | _____

"That it is," Reverend John agreed. "But we must remember | 207 | _____

this war is far from over." | 213 | _____

Needs Work   1   2   3   4   5   Excellent
Paid attention to punctuation

Needs Work   1   2   3   4   5   Excellent
Sounded good

Total Words Read   _____

Total Errors − _____

Correct WPM   _____

8

Fiction

from **"Rip Van Winkle"**
by Washington Irving

Imagine Rip Van Winkle's confusion after waking from a
20-year nap.

	Words Read	Miscues

As he arose to walk he found himself stiff in the joints, and | 13 | _____
wanting in his usual activity. "These mountain beds do not agree | 24 | _____
with me," thought Rip, "and if this frolic should lay me up with a | 38 | _____
fit of the rheumatism, I shall have a blessed time with Dame Van | 51 | _____
Winkle." With some difficulty he got down into the glen: he | 62 | _____
found the gully up which he and his companion had ascended the | 74 | _____
preceding evening, but to his astonishment a mountain stream | 83 | _____
was now foaming down it, leaping from rock to rock, and filling | 95 | _____
the glen with babbling murmurs. He, however, made shift to | 105 | _____
scramble up its sides, working his toilsome way through thickets | 115 | _____
of birch, sassafras, and witch hazel, and sometimes tripped up | 125 | _____
or entangled by the wild grape vines that twisted their coils | 136 | _____
and tendrils from tree to tree, and spread a kind of network in | 149 | _____
his path. | 151 | _____

At length he reached to where the ravine had opened through | 162 | _____
the cliffs, to the amphitheater; but no traces of such opening | 173 | _____
remained. The rocks presented a high impenetrable wall, over | 182 | _____
which the torrent came tumbling in a sheet of feathery foam, and | 194 | _____
fell into a broad deep basin, black from the shadows of the | 206 | _____
surrounding forest. | 208 | _____

Needs Work   1 2 3 4 5   Excellent
Paid attention to punctuation

Needs Work   1 2 3 4 5   Excellent
Sounded good

Total Words Read _____

Total Errors − _____

Correct WPM _____

8
Fiction

from "**Rip Van Winkle**"
by Washington Irving

Imagine Rip Van Winkle's confusion after waking from a
20-year nap.

	Words Read	Miscues
As he arose to walk he found himself stiff in the joints, and	13	_____
wanting in his usual activity. "These mountain beds do not agree	24	_____
with me," thought Rip, "and if this frolic should lay me up with a	38	_____
fit of the rheumatism, I shall have a blessed time with Dame Van	51	_____
Winkle." With some difficulty he got down into the glen: he	62	_____
found the gully up which he and his companion had ascended the	74	_____
preceding evening, but to his astonishment a mountain stream	83	_____
was now foaming down it, leaping from rock to rock, and filling	95	_____
the glen with babbling murmurs. He, however, made shift to	105	_____
scramble up its sides, working his toilsome way through thickets	115	_____
of birch, sassafras, and witch hazel, and sometimes tripped up	125	_____
or entangled by the wild grape vines that twisted their coils	136	_____
and tendrils from tree to tree, and spread a kind of network in	149	_____
his path.	151	_____
At length he reached to where the ravine had opened through	162	_____
the cliffs, to the amphitheater; but no traces of such opening	173	_____
remained. The rocks presented a high impenetrable wall, over	182	_____
which the torrent came tumbling in a sheet of feathery foam, and	194	_____
fell into a broad deep basin, black from the shadows of the	206	_____
surrounding forest.	208	_____

Needs Work   1 2 3 4 5   Excellent
_____
Paid attention to punctuation

Needs Work   1 2 3 4 5   Excellent
_____
Sounded good

Total Words Read   _____

Total Errors − _____

Correct WPM   _____

9

Nonfiction

from "The Crisis, No. 1"
by Thomas Paine

Read the opening of Paine's 1776 statement seeking to stir up
revolutionary spirit in the colonies.

First Reading

	Words Read	Miscues

These are the times that try men's souls. The summer soldier | 11 | _____

and the sunshine patriot will, in this crisis, shrink from the service | 23 | _____

of their country; but he that stands it now, deserves the love and | 36 | _____

thanks of man and woman. Tyranny, like hell, is not easily | 47 | _____

conquered; yet we have this consolation with us, that the harder | 58 | _____

the conflict, the more glorious the triumph. What we obtain too | 69 | _____

cheap, we esteem too lightly: it is dearness only that gives | 80 | _____

everything its value. Heaven knows how to put a proper price | 91 | _____

upon its goods; and it would be strange indeed if so celestial an | 104 | _____

article as freedom should not be highly rated. Britain, with an | 115 | _____

army to enforce her tyranny, has declared that she has a right | 127 | _____

(not only to tax) but "to bind us in all cases whatsoever," and if | 141 | _____

being bound in that manner is not slavery, then is there not such | 154 | _____

a thing as slavery upon earth. Even the expression is impious; for | 166 | _____

so unlimited a power can belong only to God. | 175 | _____

Whether the independence of the continent was declared | 183 | _____

too soon, or delayed too long, I will not now enter into as an | 197 | _____

argument; my own simple opinion is that had it been eight | 208 | _____

months earlier, it would have been much better. | 216 | _____

Needs Work   1 2 3 4 5   Excellent
Paid attention to punctuation

Needs Work   1 2 3 4 5   Excellent
Sounded good

Total Words Read   _____

Total Errors   − _____

Correct WPM   _____

9

Nonfiction

from "The Crisis, No. 1"

by Thomas Paine

Read the opening of Paine's 1776 statement seeking to stir up
revolutionary spirit in the colonies.

Second Reading

	Words Read	Miscues

These are the times that try men's souls. The summer soldier | 11 | _____
and the sunshine patriot will, in this crisis, shrink from the service | 23 | _____
of their country; but he that stands it now, deserves the love and | 36 | _____
thanks of man and woman. Tyranny, like hell, is not easily | 47 | _____
conquered; yet we have this consolation with us, that the harder | 58 | _____
the conflict, the more glorious the triumph. What we obtain too | 69 | _____
cheap, we esteem too lightly: it is dearness only that gives | 80 | _____
everything its value. Heaven knows how to put a proper price | 91 | _____
upon its goods; and it would be strange indeed if so celestial an | 104 | _____
article as freedom should not be highly rated. Britain, with an | 115 | _____
army to enforce her tyranny, has declared that she has a right | 127 | _____
(not only to tax) but "to bind us in all cases whatsoever," and if | 141 | _____
being bound in that manner is not slavery, then is there not such | 154 | _____
a thing as slavery upon earth. Even the expression is impious; for | 166 | _____
so unlimited a power can belong only to God. | 175 | _____

Whether the independence of the continent was declared | 183 | _____
too soon, or delayed too long, I will not now enter into as an | 197 | _____
argument; my own simple opinion is that had it been eight | 208 | _____
months earlier, it would have been much better. | 216 | _____

Needs Work   1   2   3   4   5   Excellent
Paid attention to punctuation

Needs Work   1   2   3   4   5   Excellent
Sounded good

Total Words Read _____

Total Errors − _____

Correct WPM _____

10

Nonfiction

from *Kaffir Boy*
by Mark Mathabane

First Reading

Listen as the narrator describes one example of racial discrimination toward children in South Africa.

	Words Read	Miscues

A million times I wondered why the sparse library at my tribal — 12

school did not carry books like *Treasure Island*, why most of the — 24

books we read had tribal points of view. I would ask teachers and — 37

would be told that under the Bantu Education law black children — 48

were supposed to acquire a solid foundation in tribal life, which — 59

would prepare them for a productive future in their respective — 69

homelands. In this way the dream of Dr. Verwoerd, prime — 79

minister of South Africa and the architect of Bantu Education, — 89

would be realized, for he insisted that "the native child must be — 101

taught subjects which will enable him to work with and among — 112

his own people; therefore there is no use misleading him by — 123

showing him the green pastures of European society, in which he — 134

is not allowed to graze. Bantu Education should not be used to — 146

create imitation whites." — 149

How I cursed Dr. Verwoerd and his law for prescribing how I — 161

should feel and think. I started looking toward the Smiths to — 172

provide me with the books about a different reality. Each day — 183

Granny came back from work around five in the afternoon, I — 194

would be the first to meet her at the gate, always with the same — 208

question, "Any books for me today?" — 214

Needs Work   1   2   3   4   5   Excellent
Paid attention to punctuation

Needs Work   1   2   3   4   5   Excellent
Sounded good

Total Words Read _____

Total Errors − _____

Correct WPM _____

from *Kaffir Boy*

by Mark Mathabane

Listen as the narrator describes one example of racial discrimination toward children in South Africa.

	Words Read	Miscues

A million times I wondered why the sparse library at my tribal | 12 | _____

school did not carry books like *Treasure Island*, why most of the | 24 | _____

books we read had tribal points of view. I would ask teachers and | 37 | _____

would be told that under the Bantu Education law black children | 48 | _____

were supposed to acquire a solid foundation in tribal life, which | 59 | _____

would prepare them for a productive future in their respective | 69 | _____

homelands. In this way the dream of Dr. Verwoerd, prime | 79 | _____

minister of South Africa and the architect of Bantu Education, | 89 | _____

would be realized, for he insisted that "the native child must be | 101 | _____

taught subjects which will enable him to work with and among | 112 | _____

his own people; therefore there is no use misleading him by | 123 | _____

showing him the green pastures of European society, in which he | 134 | _____

is not allowed to graze. Bantu Education should not be used to | 146 | _____

create imitation whites." | 149 | _____

How I cursed Dr. Verwoerd and his law for prescribing how I | 161 | _____

should feel and think. I started looking toward the Smiths to | 172 | _____

provide me with the books about a different reality. Each day | 183 | _____

Granny came back from work around five in the afternoon, I | 194 | _____

would be the first to meet her at the gate, always with the same | 208 | _____

question, "Any books for me today?" | 214 | _____

Needs Work   1   2   3   4   5   Excellent
Paid attention to punctuation

Needs Work   1   2   3   4   5   Excellent
Sounded good

Total Words Read _____

Total Errors − _____

Correct WPM _____

11
Fiction

from *My Ántonia*
by Willa Cather

Read about a family in the early 1900s traveling to a new home
in an unfamiliar place.

	Words Read	Miscues
We went all the way in day-coaches, becoming more sticky	10	_____
and grimy with each stage of the journey. Jake bought everything	21	_____
the newsboys offered him: candy, oranges, brass collar buttons, a	31	_____
watch-charm, and for me a "Life of Jesse James," which I	42	_____
remember as one of the most satisfactory books I have ever read.	54	_____
Beyond Chicago we were under the protection of a friendly	64	_____
passenger conductor, who knew all about the country to which we	75	_____
were going and gave us a great deal of advice in exchange for our	89	_____
confidence. He seemed to us an experienced and worldly man	99	_____
who had been almost everywhere; in his conversation he threw	109	_____
out lightly the names of distant states and cities. He wore the	121	_____
rings and pins and badges of different fraternal orders to which	132	_____
he belonged. Even his cuff-buttons were engraved with	140	_____
hieroglyphics, and he was more inscribed than an Egyptian	149	_____
obelisk. Once when he sat down to chat, he told us that in the	163	_____
immigrant car ahead there was a family from "across the water"	174	_____
whose destination was the same as ours.	181	_____
"They can't any of them speak English, except one little girl,	192	_____
and all she can say is 'We go Black Hawk, Nebraska.'"	203	_____

Needs Work   1 2 3 4 5   Excellent
Paid attention to punctuation

Needs Work   1 2 3 4 5   Excellent
Sounded good

Total Words Read _____

Total Errors − _____

Correct WPM _____

11

from *My Ántonia*

by Willa Cather

Read about a family in the early 1900s traveling to a new home in an unfamiliar place.

	Words Read	Miscues
We went all the way in day-coaches, becoming more sticky	10	_____
and grimy with each stage of the journey. Jake bought everything	21	_____
the newsboys offered him: candy, oranges, brass collar buttons, a	31	_____
watch-charm, and for me a "Life of Jesse James," which I	42	_____
remember as one of the most satisfactory books I have ever read.	54	_____
Beyond Chicago we were under the protection of a friendly	64	_____
passenger conductor, who knew all about the country to which we	75	_____
were going and gave us a great deal of advice in exchange for our	89	_____
confidence. He seemed to us an experienced and worldly man	99	_____
who had been almost everywhere; in his conversation he threw	109	_____
out lightly the names of distant states and cities. He wore the	121	_____
rings and pins and badges of different fraternal orders to which	132	_____
he belonged. Even his cuff-buttons were engraved with	140	_____
hieroglyphics, and he was more inscribed than an Egyptian	149	_____
obelisk. Once when he sat down to chat, he told us that in the	163	_____
immigrant car ahead there was a family from "across the water"	174	_____
whose destination was the same as ours.	181	_____
"They can't any of them speak English, except one little girl,	192	_____
and all she can say is 'We go Black Hawk, Nebraska.'"	203	_____

Needs Work 1 2 3 4 5 Excellent
Paid attention to punctuation

Needs Work 1 2 3 4 5 Excellent
Sounded good

Total Words Read _____

Total Errors −_____

Correct WPM _____

12

from *Act One*
by Moss Hart

Take a taxicab ride with playwright Moss Hart on the morning after
his first Broadway success.

First Reading

	Words Read	Miscues

I waved at Joe Hyman through the rear window until the cab   12   _____

turned the corner, and then settled back in the seat, determined   23   _____

that I would not fall asleep. I had no intention of dozing through   36   _____

the first ride to Brooklyn above ground—I intended to enjoy   47   _____

every visible moment of it and I very shortly reaped the reward   59   _____

for staying awake.   62   _____

No one has ever seen the skyline of the city from Brooklyn   74   _____

Bridge as I saw it that morning with three hit notices under my   87   _____

arm. The face of the city is always invested with grandeur, but   99   _____

grandeur can be chilling. The overpowering symmetry of that   108   _____

skyline can crush the spirit and make the city seem forbidding   119   _____

and impenetrable, but today it seemed to emerge from cold   129   _____

anonymity and grant its acknowledgment and acceptance. There   137   _____

was no sunlight—it was a gray day and the buildings were half   150   _____

shrouded in mist, but it was a city that would know my name   163   _____

today, a city that had not turned me aside, and a city that I loved.   178   _____

Unexpectedly and without warning a great wave of feeling for this   189   _____

proud and beautiful city swept over me.   196   _____

Needs Work   1   2   3   4   5   Excellent
Paid attention to punctuation

Needs Work   1   2   3   4   5   Excellent
Sounded good

Total Words Read _____

Total Errors − _____

Correct WPM _____

from *Act One*

by Moss Hart

Take a taxicab ride with playwright Moss Hart on the morning after
his first Broadway success.

Second Reading

	Words Read	Miscues

I waved at Joe Hyman through the rear window until the cab — 12 _____

turned the corner, and then settled back in the seat, determined — 23 _____

that I would not fall asleep. I had no intention of dozing through — 36 _____

the first ride to Brooklyn above ground—I intended to enjoy — 47 _____

every visible moment of it and I very shortly reaped the reward — 59 _____

for staying awake. — 62 _____

No one has ever seen the skyline of the city from Brooklyn — 74 _____

Bridge as I saw it that morning with three hit notices under my — 87 _____

arm. The face of the city is always invested with grandeur, but — 99 _____

grandeur can be chilling. The overpowering symmetry of that — 108 _____

skyline can crush the spirit and make the city seem forbidding — 119 _____

and impenetrable, but today it seemed to emerge from cold — 129 _____

anonymity and grant its acknowledgment and acceptance. There — 137 _____

was no sunlight—it was a gray day and the buildings were half — 150 _____

shrouded in mist, but it was a city that would know my name — 163 _____

today, a city that had not turned me aside, and a city that I loved. — 178 _____

Unexpectedly and without warning a great wave of feeling for this — 189 _____

proud and beautiful city swept over me. — 196 _____

Needs Work   1   2   3   4   5   Excellent
Paid attention to punctuation

Needs Work   1   2   3   4   5   Excellent
Sounded good

Total Words Read _____

Total Errors − _____

Correct WPM _____

13

Fiction

from *Sometimes a Great Notion*
by Ken Kesey

Find out what often happens to older houses that are built
on riverbanks.

First Reading

	Words Read	Miscues

Draeger bends his big Pontiac around the riverside curves,   9 _____

feeling feverish and mellow and well fed, with a sense of recent   21 _____

accomplishments, listlessly musing about a peculiarity that the   29 _____

very house he muses about would find not the least bit peculiar.   41 _____

The houses know about riverside living. Even the modern   50 _____

weekend summertime places have learned. The old houses, the   59 _____

very old houses that were built of cedar shake and lodgepole by   71 _____

the first settlers at the turn of the eighteen-hundreds, were long   82 _____

ago jacked up and dragged back from the bank by borrowed   93 _____

teams of horses and logging oxen. Or, if they were too big to   106 _____

move, were abandoned to tip headlong into the water as the river   118 _____

sucked away the foundations.   122 _____

Many of the settlers' houses were lost this way. They had all   134 _____

wanted to build along the river's edge in those first years, for   146 _____

convenience's sake, to be close to their transportation, their   155 _____

"Highway of Water," as the river is referred to frequently in   166 _____

yellowed newspapers in the Wakonda Library. The settlers had   175 _____

hurried to claim banksite lots, not knowing at first that their   186 _____

highway had a habit of eating away its banks and all that those   199 _____

banks might hold.   202 _____

Needs Work   1   2   3   4   5   Excellent
      Paid attention to punctuation

Needs Work   1   2   3   4   5   Excellent
      Sounded good

Total Words Read   _____

Total Errors   − _____

Correct WPM   _____

13

Fiction

from *Sometimes a Great Notion*

by Ken Kesey

Find out what often happens to older houses that are built on riverbanks.

	Words Read	Miscues

Draeger bends his big Pontiac around the riverside curves, | 9 | _____ |
feeling feverish and mellow and well fed, with a sense of recent | 21 | _____ |
accomplishments, listlessly musing about a peculiarity that the | 29 | _____ |
very house he muses about would find not the least bit peculiar. | 41 | _____ |
The houses know about riverside living. Even the modern | 50 | _____ |
weekend summertime places have learned. The old houses, the | 59 | _____ |
very old houses that were built of cedar shake and lodgepole by | 71 | _____ |
the first settlers at the turn of the eighteen-hundreds, were long | 82 | _____ |
ago jacked up and dragged back from the bank by borrowed | 93 | _____ |
teams of horses and logging oxen. Or, if they were too big to | 106 | _____ |
move, were abandoned to tip headlong into the water as the river | 118 | _____ |
sucked away the foundations. | 122 | _____ |

Many of the settlers' houses were lost this way. They had all | 134 | _____ |
wanted to build along the river's edge in those first years, for | 146 | _____ |
convenience's sake, to be close to their transportation, their | 155 | _____ |
"Highway of Water," as the river is referred to frequently in | 166 | _____ |
yellowed newspapers in the Wakonda Library. The settlers had | 175 | _____ |
hurried to claim banksite lots, not knowing at first that their | 186 | _____ |
highway had a habit of eating away its banks and all that those | 199 | _____ |
banks might hold. | 202 | _____ |

Needs Work   1   2   3   4   5   Excellent
_____
Paid attention to punctuation

Needs Work   1   2   3   4   5   Excellent
_____
Sounded good

Total Words Read   _____

Total Errors − _____

Correct WPM   _____

14 from *The Street*

Fiction   by Ann Petry

Read this vivid description of an urban scene, which begins
Ann Petry's novel.

First Reading

	Words Read	Miscues

There was a cold November wind blowing through 116th | 9 | _____

Street. It rattled the tops of garbage cans, sucked window shades | 20 | _____

out through the top of opened windows and set them flapping | 31 | _____

back against the windows; and it drove most of the people off the | 44 | _____

street in the block between Seventh and Eighth Avenues except | 54 | _____

for a few hurried pedestrians who bent double in an effort to | 66 | _____

offer the least possible exposed surface to its violent assault. | 76 | _____

It found every scrap of paper along the street—theater | 86 | _____

throwaways, announcements of dances and lodge meetings, the | 94 | _____

heavy waxed paper that loaves of bread had been wrapped in, the | 106 | _____

thinner waxed paper that had enclosed sandwiches, old envelopes, | 115 | _____

newspapers. Fingering its way along the curb, the wind set the | 126 | _____

bits of paper to dancing high in the air, so that a barrage of paper | 141 | _____

swirled into the faces of the people on the street. It even took | 154 | _____

time to rush into doorways and areaways and find chicken bones | 165 | _____

and pork-chop bones and pushed them along the curb. | 174 | _____

It did everything it could to discourage the people walking | 184 | _____

along the street. It found all the dirt and dust and grime on the | 198 | _____

sidewalk and lifted it up so that the dirt got into their noses, | 211 | _____

making it difficult to breathe. | 216 | _____

Needs Work   1 2 3 4 5   Excellent
 Paid attention to punctuation

Needs Work   1 2 3 4 5   Excellent
 Sounded good

Total Words Read _____

Total Errors − _____

Correct WPM _____

from *The Street*

by Ann Petry

Read this vivid description of an urban scene, which begins
Ann Petry's novel.

	Words Read	Miscues
There was a cold November wind blowing through 116th	9	_____
Street. It rattled the tops of garbage cans, sucked window shades	20	_____
out through the top of opened windows and set them flapping	31	_____
back against the windows; and it drove most of the people off the	44	_____
street in the block between Seventh and Eighth Avenues except	54	_____
for a few hurried pedestrians who bent double in an effort to	66	_____
offer the least possible exposed surface to its violent assault.	76	_____
It found every scrap of paper along the street—theater	86	_____
throwaways, announcements of dances and lodge meetings, the	94	_____
heavy waxed paper that loaves of bread had been wrapped in, the	106	_____
thinner waxed paper that had enclosed sandwiches, old envelopes,	115	_____
newspapers. Fingering its way along the curb, the wind set the	126	_____
bits of paper to dancing high in the air, so that a barrage of paper	141	_____
swirled into the faces of the people on the street. It even took	154	_____
time to rush into doorways and areaways and find chicken bones	165	_____
and pork-chop bones and pushed them along the curb.	174	_____
It did everything it could to discourage the people walking	184	_____
along the street. It found all the dirt and dust and grime on the	198	_____
sidewalk and lifted it up so that the dirt got into their noses,	211	_____
making it difficult to breathe.	216	_____

Needs Work 1 2 3 4 5 Excellent
Paid attention to punctuation

Needs Work 1 2 3 4 5 Excellent
Sounded good

Total Words Read _____

Total Errors − _____

Correct WPM _____

15

Fiction

from *Native Speaker*

by Chang-rae Lee

Enjoy this fond memory of a routine Sunday visit to
a Korean grocery.

First Reading

	Words Read	Miscues

I used to love to walk these streets of Flushing with Lelia and   13   _____

Mitt, bring them back here on Sunday trips during the summer.   24   _____

We would eat cold buckwheat noodles at a Korean restaurant   34   _____

near the subway station and then go browsing in the big Korean   46   _____

groceries, not corner vegetable stands like my father's but real   56   _____

supermarkets with every kind of Asian food. Mitt always marveled   66   _____

at the long wall of glassed-door refrigerators stacked full with   76   _____

gallon jars of five kinds of kimchee, and even he noticed that if a   90   _____

customer took one down the space was almost immediately filled   100   _____

with another. *The kimchee museum*, he'd say, with appropriate awe.   110   _____

Then, Lelia would stray off to the butcher's section, Mitt to the   122   _____

candies. I always went to the back, to the magazine section, and   134   _____

although I couldn't read the Korean well I'd pretend anyway, just   145   _____

as I did when I was a boy, flipping the pages from right to left, my   161   _____

finger scanning vertically the way my father read. Eventually I'd   171   _____

hear Lelia's voice, calling to both of us, calling the only English to   184   _____

be heard that day in the store, and we would meet again at the   198   _____

register with what we wanted.   203   _____

Needs Work   1   2   3   4   5   Excellent
Paid attention to punctuation

Needs Work   1   2   3   4   5   Excellent
Sounded good

Total Words Read   _____

Total Errors – _____

Correct WPM   _____

from *Native Speaker*

by Chang-rae Lee

Enjoy this fond memory of a routine Sunday visit to
a Korean grocery.

	Words Read	Miscues

I used to love to walk these streets of Flushing with Lelia and | 13 | _____

Mitt, bring them back here on Sunday trips during the summer. | 24 | _____

We would eat cold buckwheat noodles at a Korean restaurant | 34 | _____

near the subway station and then go browsing in the big Korean | 46 | _____

groceries, not corner vegetable stands like my father's but real | 56 | _____

supermarkets with every kind of Asian food. Mitt always marveled | 66 | _____

at the long wall of glassed-door refrigerators stacked full with | 76 | _____

gallon jars of five kinds of kimchee, and even he noticed that if a | 90 | _____

customer took one down the space was almost immediately filled | 100 | _____

with another. *The kimchee museum*, he'd say, with appropriate awe. | 110 | _____

Then, Lelia would stray off to the butcher's section, Mitt to the | 122 | _____

candies. I always went to the back, to the magazine section, and | 134 | _____

although I couldn't read the Korean well I'd pretend anyway, just | 145 | _____

as I did when I was a boy, flipping the pages from right to left, my | 161 | _____

finger scanning vertically the way my father read. Eventually I'd | 171 | _____

hear Lelia's voice, calling to both of us, calling the only English to | 184 | _____

be heard that day in the store, and we would meet again at the | 198 | _____

register with what we wanted. | 203 | _____

Needs Work   1   2   3   4   5   Excellent
  Paid attention to punctuation

Needs Work   1   2   3   4   5   Excellent
  Sounded good

Total Words Read _____

Total Errors − _____

Correct WPM _____

16

Fiction

from *Around the World in Eighty Days*

by Jules Verne

Consider how differently the two men regard the stormy sea that threatens to delay their journey.

First Reading

	Words Read	Miscues

Phileas Fogg gazed at the tempestuous sea, which seemed to — 10 — _____

be struggling especially to delay him, with his habitual tranquility. — 20 — _____

He never changed countenance for an instant, though a delay of — 31 — _____

twenty hours, by making him too late for the Yokohama boat, — 42 — _____

would almost inevitably cause the loss of the wager. But this man — 54 — _____

of nerve manifested neither impatience nor annoyance; it seemed — 63 — _____

as if the storm were a part of his program, and had been foreseen. — 77 — _____

Aouda was amazed to find him as calm as he had been from the — 91 — _____

first time she saw him. — 96 — _____

Mr. Fix did not look at the state of things in the same light. — 110 — _____

The storm greatly pleased him. His satisfaction would have been — 120 — _____

complete had their boat, *Rangoon*, been forced to retreat before — 130 — _____

the violence of wind and waves. Each delay filled him with hope, — 142 — _____

for it became more and more probable that Fogg would be — 153 — _____

obliged to remain some days at Hong Kong; and now the heavens — 164 — _____

themselves became his allies, with the gusts and squalls. It — 174 — _____

mattered not that they made him seasick—he made no account of — 186 — _____

this inconvenience; and while his body was writhing under their — 196 — _____

effects, his spirit bounded with hopeful exultation. — 203 — _____

Needs Work   1   2   3   4   5   Excellent
Paid attention to punctuation

Needs Work   1   2   3   4   5   Excellent
Sounded good

Total Words Read _____

Total Errors − _____

Correct WPM _____

from *Around the World in Eighty Days*

by Jules Verne

Consider how differently the two men regard the stormy sea that threatens to delay their journey.

	Words Read	Miscues
Phileas Fogg gazed at the tempestuous sea, which seemed to	10	_____
be struggling especially to delay him, with his habitual tranquility.	20	_____
He never changed countenance for an instant, though a delay of	31	_____
twenty hours, by making him too late for the Yokohama boat,	42	_____
would almost inevitably cause the loss of the wager. But this man	54	_____
of nerve manifested neither impatience nor annoyance; it seemed	63	_____
as if the storm were a part of his program, and had been foreseen.	77	_____
Aouda was amazed to find him as calm as he had been from the	91	_____
first time she saw him.	96	_____
Mr. Fix did not look at the state of things in the same light.	110	_____
The storm greatly pleased him. His satisfaction would have been	120	_____
complete had their boat, *Rangoon*, been forced to retreat before	130	_____
the violence of wind and waves. Each delay filled him with hope,	142	_____
for it became more and more probable that Fogg would be	153	_____
obliged to remain some days at Hong Kong; and now the heavens	164	_____
themselves became his allies, with the gusts and squalls. It	174	_____
mattered not that they made him seasick—he made no account of	186	_____
this inconvenience; and while his body was writhing under their	196	_____
effects, his spirit bounded with hopeful exultation.	203	_____

Needs Work   1   2   3   4   5   Excellent
Paid attention to punctuation

Needs Work   1   2   3   4   5   Excellent
Sounded good

Total Words Read   _____

Total Errors − _____

Correct WPM   _____

17

Fiction

from *Ivanhoe*
by Sir Walter Scott

Discover how spectators and contestants prepared for a jousting tournament in medieval England.

First Reading

	Words Read	Miscues

The Prince marshalled Rowena to the seat of honor opposite — 10 —

his own, while the fairest and most distinguished ladies present — 20 —

crowded after her to obtain places as near as possible to their — 32 —

temporary sovereign. — 34 —

No sooner was Rowena seated, than a burst of music, — 44 —

half-drowned by the shouts of the multitude, greeted her new — 54 —

dignity. Meantime, the sun shone fierce and bright upon the — 64 —

polished arms of the knights of either side, who crowded the — 75 —

opposite extremities of the lists, and held eager conference — 84 —

together concerning the best mode of arranging their line of — 94 —

battle, and supporting the conflict. — 99 —

The heralds then proclaimed silence until the laws of the — 109 —

tourney should be rehearsed. These were calculated in some — 118 —

degree to abate the dangers of the day; a precaution the more — 130 —

necessary as the conflict was to be maintained with sharp swords — 141 —

and pointed lances. — 144 —

The champions were therefore prohibited to thrust with the — 153 —

sword, and were confined to striking. A knight, it was announced, — 164 —

might use a mace or battle-axe at pleasure, but the dagger was a — 177 —

prohibited weapon. A knight unhorsed might renew the fight on — 187 —

foot with any other on the opposite side in the same predicament; — 199 —

but mounted horsemen were in that case forbidden to assail him. — 210 —

Needs Work   1   2   3   4   5   Excellent
Paid attention to punctuation

Needs Work   1   2   3   4   5   Excellent
Sounded good

Total Words Read _____

Total Errors − _____

Correct WPM _____

17

Fiction

from *Ivanhoe*
by Sir Walter Scott

Discover how spectators and contestants prepared for a jousting tournament in medieval England.

	Words Read	Miscues

The Prince marshalled Rowena to the seat of honor opposite | 10 | _____

his own, while the fairest and most distinguished ladies present | 20 | _____

crowded after her to obtain places as near as possible to their | 32 | _____

temporary sovereign. | 34 | _____

No sooner was Rowena seated, than a burst of music, | 44 | _____

half-drowned by the shouts of the multitude, greeted her new | 54 | _____

dignity. Meantime, the sun shone fierce and bright upon the | 64 | _____

polished arms of the knights of either side, who crowded the | 75 | _____

opposite extremities of the lists, and held eager conference | 84 | _____

together concerning the best mode of arranging their line of | 94 | _____

battle, and supporting the conflict. | 99 | _____

The heralds then proclaimed silence until the laws of the | 109 | _____

tourney should be rehearsed. These were calculated in some | 118 | _____

degree to abate the dangers of the day; a precaution the more | 130 | _____

necessary as the conflict was to be maintained with sharp swords | 141 | _____

and pointed lances. | 144 | _____

The champions were therefore prohibited to thrust with the | 153 | _____

sword, and were confined to striking. A knight, it was announced, | 164 | _____

might use a mace or battle-axe at pleasure, but the dagger was a | 177 | _____

prohibited weapon. A knight unhorsed might renew the fight on | 187 | _____

foot with any other on the opposite side in the same predicament; | 199 | _____

but mounted horsemen were in that case forbidden to assail him. | 210 | _____

Needs Work 1 2 3 4 5 Excellent
Paid attention to punctuation

Needs Work 1 2 3 4 5 Excellent
Sounded good

Total Words Read _____

Total Errors − _____

Correct WPM _____

18

Nonfiction

from *The Hot Zone*
by Richard Preston

Learn how one of the most deadly viral diseases known to humans spread from the jungles of Africa.

First Reading

	Words Read	Miscues

In the first days of September, some unknown person who — 10 _____

probably lived somewhere to the south of the Ebola River perhaps — 21 _____

touched something bloody. It might have been monkey meat— — 30 _____

people in that area hunt monkeys for food—or it might have — 42 _____

been the meat of some other animal, such as an elephant or a — 55 _____

bat. Or perhaps the person touched a crushed insect, or perhaps — 66 _____

he or she was bitten by a spider. Whatever the original host of the — 80 _____

virus, it seems that a blood-to-blood contact in the rain forest — 91 _____

enabled the virus to move into the human world. The portal into — 103 _____

the human race may well have been a cut on this unknown — 115 _____

person's hand. — 117 _____

The virus surfaced in the Yambuku Mission Hospital, an — 126 _____

upcountry clinic run by Belgian nuns. The hospital was a — 136 _____

collection of corrugated tin roofs and whitewashed concrete walls — 145 _____

sitting beside a church in the forest, where bells rang and you — 157 _____

heard a sound of hymns and the words of the high mass spoken — 170 _____

in Bantu. Next door, people stood in line at the clinic and — 182 _____

shivered with malaria while they waited for a nun to give them an — 195 _____

injection of medicine that might make them feel better. — 204 _____

Needs Work   1 2 3 4 5   Excellent
Paid attention to punctuation

Needs Work   1 2 3 4 5   Excellent
Sounded good

Total Words Read _____

Total Errors − _____

Correct WPM _____

18

Nonfiction

from *The Hot Zone*

by Richard Preston

Learn how one of the most deadly viral diseases known to
humans spread from the jungles of Africa.

	Words Read	Miscues

In the first days of September, some unknown person who probably lived somewhere to the south of the Ebola River perhaps touched something bloody. It might have been monkey meat— people in that area hunt monkeys for food—or it might have been the meat of some other animal, such as an elephant or a bat. Or perhaps the person touched a crushed insect, or perhaps he or she was bitten by a spider. Whatever the original host of the virus, it seems that a blood-to-blood contact in the rain forest enabled the virus to move into the human world. The portal into the human race may well have been a cut on this unknown person's hand.

The virus surfaced in the Yambuku Mission Hospital, an upcountry clinic run by Belgian nuns. The hospital was a collection of corrugated tin roofs and whitewashed concrete walls sitting beside a church in the forest, where bells rang and you heard a sound of hymns and the words of the high mass spoken in Bantu. Next door, people stood in line at the clinic and shivered with malaria while they waited for a nun to give them an injection of medicine that might make them feel better.

Words Read
10
21
30
42
55
66
80
91
103
115
117
126
136
145
157
170
182
195
204

Needs Work   1 2 3 4 5   Excellent
Paid attention to punctuation

Needs Work   1 2 3 4 5   Excellent
Sounded good

Total Words Read _____

Total Errors − _____

Correct WPM _____

19
Fiction
from "The Story of Prince Yamato Take"

translated by Yei Theodora Ozaki

Settle in for the beginning of this ancient tale of adventure and daring.

First Reading

	Words Read	Miscues

Once, many, many years ago, there was born a son to the   12   _____
Emperor Keiko, the twelfth in descent from the great Jimmu, the   23   _____
founder of the Japanese dynasty. This prince was the second son   34   _____
of the Emperor Keiko, and he was named Yamato. From his   45   _____
childhood he proved himself to be of remarkable strength,   54   _____
wisdom, and courage, and his father noticed with pride that he   65   _____
gave promise of great things, and he loved him even more than   77   _____
he did his elder son.   82   _____

Now when Prince Yamato had grown to manhood (in the   92   _____
olden days of Japanese history, a boy was considered to have   103   _____
reached man's estate at the early age of sixteen) the realm was   115   _____
much troubled by a band of outlaws whose chiefs were two   126   _____
brothers, Kumaso and Takeru. These rebels seemed to delight   135   _____
in rebelling against the king, in breaking the laws and defying   146   _____
all authority.   148   _____

At last King Keiko ordered his younger son Prince Yamato to   159   _____
subdue the brigands and, if possible, to rid the land of their evil   172   _____
lives. Prince Yamato was only sixteen years of age, he had but   184   _____
reached his manhood according to the law, yet though he was   195   _____
such a youth in years he possessed the dauntless spirit of a   207   _____
warrior of fuller age and knew not what fear was.   217   _____

Needs Work   1   2   3   4   5   Excellent
Paid attention to punctuation

Needs Work   1   2   3   4   5   Excellent
Sounded good

Total Words Read   _____

Total Errors   − _____

Correct WPM   _____

19

from "The Story of Prince Yamato Take"

translated by Yei Theodora Ozaki

Settle in for the beginning of this ancient tale of adventure and daring.

Second Reading

	Words Read	Miscues

Once, many, many years ago, there was born a son to the   12 _____
Emperor Keiko, the twelfth in descent from the great Jimmu, the   23 _____
founder of the Japanese dynasty. This prince was the second son   34 _____
of the Emperor Keiko, and he was named Yamato. From his   45 _____
childhood he proved himself to be of remarkable strength,   54 _____
wisdom, and courage, and his father noticed with pride that he   65 _____
gave promise of great things, and he loved him even more than   77 _____
he did his elder son.   82 _____

Now when Prince Yamato had grown to manhood (in the   92 _____
olden days of Japanese history, a boy was considered to have   103 _____
reached man's estate at the early age of sixteen) the realm was   115 _____
much troubled by a band of outlaws whose chiefs were two   126 _____
brothers, Kumaso and Takeru. These rebels seemed to delight   135 _____
in rebelling against the king, in breaking the laws and defying   146 _____
all authority.   148 _____

At last King Keiko ordered his younger son Prince Yamato to   159 _____
subdue the brigands and, if possible, to rid the land of their evil   172 _____
lives. Prince Yamato was only sixteen years of age, he had but   184 _____
reached his manhood according to the law, yet though he was   195 _____
such a youth in years he possessed the dauntless spirit of a   207 _____
warrior of fuller age and knew not what fear was.   217 _____

Needs Work   1 2 3 4 5   Excellent
  Paid attention to punctuation

Needs Work   1 2 3 4 5   Excellent
  Sounded good

Total Words Read   _____

Total Errors − _____

Correct WPM   _____

20

Nonfiction

from *A Circle of Quiet*
by Madeleine L'Engle

Laugh with the author as she recalls her son's adventures with
vocabulary building.

First Reading

	Words Read	Miscues

Our youngest child, when he first became conscious of | 9 | _____
vocabulary, often did violence to words in absurd little ways | 19 | _____
which delighted us. Hugh and I listened seriously, lest we make | 30 | _____
him self-conscious, or think we were laughing at him. We needn't | 41 | _____
have worried; he plunged into vocabulary like a sea gull into | 52 | _____
water, entirely fascinated with whatever he came up with. Even | 62 | _____
the laughter of his elder siblings did not deter him, and he is now | 76 | _____
happily malaproping in Latin, French, and German. One day, aged | 86 | _____
seven, he came home from school highly indignant because the | 96 | _____
boys' gym period had been curtailed. "We only had ten minutes | 107 | _____
of gym," he said, "and that was all anesthetics." | 116 | _____

This was not just something to laugh at; it sent me back to | 129 | _____
my own, dreaded gym periods where anesthetics rather than | 138 | _____
calisthenics would have been more than welcome. Any team I was | 149 | _____
on lost automatically; when teams were chosen, mine was the last | 160 | _____
name to be reluctantly called out, and the team which had the | 172 | _____
bad luck to get me let out uninhibited groans. I now have this | 185 | _____
emotion at my fingertips if I need it for a story I'm writing; | 198 | _____
or if I need it to comfort some child who is going through a | 212 | _____
similar experience. | 214 | _____

Needs Work   1 2 3 4 5   Excellent
Paid attention to punctuation

Needs Work   1 2 3 4 5   Excellent
Sounded good

Total Words Read   _____

Total Errors − _____

Correct WPM   _____

20

from *A Circle of Quiet*

by Madeleine L'Engle

Laugh with the author as she recalls her son's adventures with vocabulary building.

Second Reading

	Words Read	Miscues

Our youngest child, when he first became conscious of
vocabulary, often did violence to words in absurd little ways
which delighted us. Hugh and I listened seriously, lest we make
him self-conscious, or think we were laughing at him. We needn't
have worried; he plunged into vocabulary like a sea gull into
water, entirely fascinated with whatever he came up with. Even
the laughter of his elder siblings did not deter him, and he is now
happily malaproping in Latin, French, and German. One day, aged
seven, he came home from school highly indignant because the
boys' gym period had been curtailed. "We only had ten minutes
of gym," he said, "and that was all anesthetics."

This was not just something to laugh at; it sent me back to
my own, dreaded gym periods where anesthetics rather than
calisthenics would have been more than welcome. Any team
I was on lost automatically; when teams were chosen, mine was
the last name to be reluctantly called out, and the team which
had the bad luck to get me let out uninhibited groans. I now have
this emotion at my fingertips if I need it for a story I'm writing;
or if I need it to comfort some child who is going through a
similar experience.

Words Read
9
19
30
41
52
62
76
86
96
107
116
129
138
149
160
172
185
198
212
214

Needs Work   1   2   3   4   5   Excellent
Paid attention to punctuation

Needs Work   1   2   3   4   5   Excellent
Sounded good

Total Words Read _____

Total Errors − _____

Correct WPM _____

21

from *Diego Rivera*
by James Cockcroft

Learn about the childhood activities of artist Diego Rivera in this
passage taken from his biography.

First Reading

	Words Read	Miscues

Diego was an exceptionally bright and observant child who
showed early signs of artistic inclination. By the time he was four,
he was grabbing whatever pens and pencils he could find around
the house and drawing on everything—furniture, walls, loose
papers. To stop the defacement, his father covered the walls of a
room with canvas and presented his son with a box of crayons
and pencils. Diego now had his very first studio.

Dieguito, as his family called him, liked to play with trains and
other mechanical objects, taking them apart to see how they
worked and then drawing them on the walls—"my first murals"
he later called them. His fascination with rail and mining
machinery earned him the nickname the Engineer by age six. He
spent hours at Guanajuato's railroad depot. One of his earliest
drawings, made when he was only two or three, was of a
locomotive with a caboose, moving steadily uphill.

Rivera's inquisitive and argumentative nature surfaced early.
His great-aunt Vicenta, called Totota by the family, believed that
her nephew sorely needed religious training to curb his rebellious
nature. She took him to the shrine of the Virgin Mary in the same
church where his aunt Cesaria had prayed for his safe birth.

Words Read
9
21
32
41
53
65
74
86
96
107
117
128
138
150
157
164
174
184
198
209

Needs Work   1   2   3   4   5   Excellent
Paid attention to punctuation

Needs Work   1   2   3   4   5   Excellent
Sounded good

Total Words Read _____

Total Errors − _____

Correct WPM _____

from *Diego Rivera*

by James Cockcroft

Learn about the childhood activities of artist Diego Rivera in this passage taken from his biography.

	Words Read	Miscues
Diego was an exceptionally bright and observant child who	9	_____
showed early signs of artistic inclination. By the time he was four,	21	_____
he was grabbing whatever pens and pencils he could find around	32	_____
the house and drawing on everything—furniture, walls, loose	41	_____
papers. To stop the defacement, his father covered the walls of a	53	_____
room with canvas and presented his son with a box of crayons	65	_____
and pencils. Diego now had his very first studio.	74	_____
Dieguito, as his family called him, liked to play with trains and	86	_____
other mechanical objects, taking them apart to see how they	96	_____
worked and then drawing them on the walls—"my first murals"	107	_____
he later called them. His fascination with rail and mining	117	_____
machinery earned him the nickname the Engineer by age six. He	128	_____
spent hours at Guanajuato's railroad depot. One of his earliest	138	_____
drawings, made when he was only two or three, was of a	150	_____
locomotive with a caboose, moving steadily uphill.	157	_____
Rivera's inquisitive and argumentative nature surfaced early.	164	_____
His great-aunt Vicenta, called Totota by the family, believed that	174	_____
her nephew sorely needed religious training to curb his rebellious	184	_____
nature. She took him to the shrine of the Virgin Mary in the same	198	_____
church where his aunt Cesaria had prayed for his safe birth.	209	_____

Needs Work   1 2 3 4 5   Excellent
Paid attention to punctuation

Needs Work   1 2 3 4 5   Excellent
Sounded good

Total Words Read   _____

Total Errors − _____

Correct WPM   _____

22

Fiction

from "And of Clay Are We Created"

by Isabel Allende
translated by Margaret Sayers Peden

Read about a television reporter racing to cover the scene of a
devastating natural disaster.

First Reading

	Words Read	Miscues
He was one of the first to reach the scene, because while other	13	_____
reporters were fighting their way to the edges of that morass in	25	_____
jeeps, bicycles, or on foot, each getting there however he could,	36	_____
Rolf Carlé had the advantage of the television helicopter, which	46	_____
flew him over the avalanche. We watched on our screens the	57	_____
footage captured by his assistant's camera, in which he was up to	69	_____
his knees in muck, a microphone in his hand, in the midst of a	83	_____
bedlam of lost children, wounded survivors, corpses, and	91	_____
devastation. The story came to us in his calm voice. For years he	104	_____
had been a familiar figure in newscasts, reporting live at the scene	116	_____
of battles and catastrophes with awesome tenacity. Nothing could	125	_____
stop him, and I was always amazed at his equanimity in the face	138	_____
of danger and suffering; it seemed as if nothing could shake his	150	_____
fortitude or deter his curiosity. Fear seemed never to touch him,	161	_____
although he had confessed to me that he was not a courageous	173	_____
man, far from it. I believe that the lens of the camera had a	187	_____
strange effect on him; it was as if it transported him to a different	201	_____
time from which he could watch events without actually	210	_____
participating in them.	213	_____

Needs Work   1 2 3 4 5   Excellent
  Paid attention to punctuation

Needs Work   1 2 3 4 5   Excellent
  Sounded good

Total Words Read _____

Total Errors − _____

Correct WPM _____

22

Fiction

from "And of Clay Are We Created"

by Isabel Allende
translated by Margaret Sayers Peden

Read about a television reporter racing to cover the scene of a devastating natural disaster.

He was one of the first to reach the scene, because while other	13	_____
reporters were fighting their way to the edges of that morass in	25	_____
jeeps, bicycles, or on foot, each getting there however he could,	36	_____
Rolf Carlé had the advantage of the television helicopter, which	46	_____
flew him over the avalanche. We watched on our screens the	57	_____
footage captured by his assistant's camera, in which he was up to	69	_____
his knees in muck, a microphone in his hand, in the midst of a	83	_____
bedlam of lost children, wounded survivors, corpses, and	91	_____
devastation. The story came to us in his calm voice. For years he	104	_____
had been a familiar figure in newscasts, reporting live at the scene	116	_____
of battles and catastrophes with awesome tenacity. Nothing could	125	_____
stop him, and I was always amazed at his equanimity in the face	138	_____
of danger and suffering; it seemed as if nothing could shake his	150	_____
fortitude or deter his curiosity. Fear seemed never to touch him,	161	_____
although he had confessed to me that he was not a courageous	173	_____
man, far from it. I believe that the lens of the camera had a	187	_____
strange effect on him; it was as if it transported him to a different	201	_____
time from which he could watch events without actually	210	_____
participating in them.	213	_____

Needs Work   1   2   3   4   5   Excellent
　　　　Paid attention to punctuation

Needs Work   1   2   3   4   5   Excellent
　　　　Sounded good

Total Words Read   _____

Total Errors   − _____

Correct WPM   _____

23 from *Gulliver's Travels*

Fiction   by Jonathan Swift

Imagine Gulliver in the land of giant people, encountering a dwarf
who is taller than he is!

First Reading

	Words Read	Miscues

Nothing angered and mortified me so much as the queen's **10** _____

dwarf; who being of the lowest stature that was ever in that **22** _____

country (for I verily think he was not full thirty feet high), became **35** _____

so insolent at seeing a creature so much beneath him, that he **47** _____

would always affect to swagger and look big as he passed by me **60** _____

in the queen's antechamber, while I was standing on some table **71** _____

talking with the lords or ladies of the court; and he seldom failed **84** _____

of a smart word or two upon my littleness; against which I could **97** _____

only revenge myself by calling him brother, challenging him to **107** _____

wrestle; and such repartees as are usually in the mouths of court **119** _____

pages. One day at dinner, this malicious little cub was so nettled **131** _____

with something I had said to him, that raising himself upon the **143** _____

frame of her Majesty's chair, he took me up by the middle, as I **157** _____

was sitting down, not thinking any harm, and let me drop into a **170** _____

large silver bowl of cream; and then ran away as fast as he could. **184** _____

I fell over head and ears, and if I had not been a good swimmer, **199** _____

it might have gone very hard with me. **207** _____

Needs Work 1 2 3 4 5 Excellent
_____
Paid attention to punctuation

Needs Work 1 2 3 4 5 Excellent
_____
Sounded good

Total Words Read _____

Total Errors − _____

Correct WPM _____

23

Fiction

from *Gulliver's Travels*

by Jonathan Swift

Imagine Gulliver in the land of giant people, encountering a dwarf
who is taller than he is!

Nothing angered and mortified me so much as the queen's	10
dwarf; who being of the lowest stature that was ever in that	22
country (for I verily think he was not full thirty feet high), became	35
so insolent at seeing a creature so much beneath him, that he	47
would always affect to swagger and look big as he passed by me	60
in the queen's antechamber, while I was standing on some table	71
talking with the lords or ladies of the court; and he seldom failed	84
of a smart word or two upon my littleness; against which I could	97
only revenge myself by calling him brother, challenging him to	107
wrestle; and such repartees as are usually in the mouths of court	119
pages. One day at dinner, this malicious little cub was so nettled	131
with something I had said to him, that raising himself upon the	143
frame of her Majesty's chair, he took me up by the middle, as I	157
was sitting down, not thinking any harm, and let me drop into a	170
large silver bowl of cream; and then ran away as fast as he could.	184
I fell over head and ears, and if I had not been a good swimmer,	199
it might have gone very hard with me.	207

Needs Work 1 2 3 4 5 Excellent
Paid attention to punctuation

Needs Work 1 2 3 4 5 Excellent
Sounded good

Total Words Read _____

Total Errors – _____

Correct WPM _____

24
Nonfiction

from *Train Go Sorry:*
Inside a Deaf World
by Leah Hager Cohen

Learn about an experiment with a hearing child studying and playing in the world of deaf children.

First Reading

	Words Read	Miscues

I played at signing the way other children play dress–up; part of trying on possibilities, practicing for the future, it was laden with excitement and anticipation, even aspiration. I wanted to grow up and be deaf, be a Lexington student, with all the accouterments: hearing aids, speech lessons, fast and clever hands.

When I was four and five years old, I was one of a few hearing children who attended Lexington's preschool as part of an experiment with integration. In many ways I seemed no different from any of my classmates, making doll cakes in the sandbox, playing chase outside on the patio, eating just the middles of my bread-and-butter snack, as was our fashion. But I was not the same.

One afternoon, while playing with my classmates outside, I sought to remedy my most blatant difference. I selected two pebbles—urban pebbles, rough bits of dark gravel—from the ground and set them in the shallow cups of cartilage above my earlobes. When the teacher spied my improvised hearing aids, I was thoroughly scolded. "Never put *anything* smaller than your elbow in your ear!" was her mystifying admonishment. Puzzling over this helped deflect some of my embarrassment and hurt, but it did nothing to help me fit in with the others.

Words Read
11
22
31
43
52
68
76
87
98
108
117
123
132
142
152
164
174
183
192
203
214

Needs Work   1   2   3   4   5   Excellent
Paid attention to punctuation

Needs Work   1   2   3   4   5   Excellent
Sounded good

Total Words Read _____

Total Errors − _____

Correct WPM _____

from *Train Go Sorry:*
Inside a Deaf World
by Leah Hager Cohen

Learn about an experiment with a hearing child studying and playing in the world of deaf children.

I played at signing the way other children play dress-up; part	11	_____
of trying on possibilities, practicing for the future, it was laden	22	_____
with excitement and anticipation, even aspiration. I wanted to	31	_____
grow up and be deaf, be a Lexington student, with all the	43	_____
accouterments: hearing aids, speech lessons, fast and clever hands.	52	_____
When I was four and five years old, I was one of a few	68	_____
hearing children who attended Lexington's preschool as part	76	_____
of an experiment with integration. In many ways I seemed no	87	_____
different from any of my classmates, making doll cakes in the	98	_____
sandbox, playing chase outside on the patio, eating just the	108	_____
middles of my bread-and-butter snack, as was our fashion.	117	_____
But I was not the same.	123	_____
One afternoon, while playing with my classmates outside, I	132	_____
sought to remedy my most blatant difference. I selected two	142	_____
pebbles—urban pebbles, rough bits of dark gravel—from the	152	_____
ground and set them in the shallow cups of cartilage above my	164	_____
earlobes. When the teacher spied my improvised hearing aids, I	174	_____
was thoroughly scolded. "Never put *anything* smaller than your	183	_____
elbow in your ear!" was her mystifying admonishment. Puzzling	192	_____
over this helped deflect some of my embarrassment and hurt, but	203	_____
it did nothing to help me fit in with the others.	214	_____

Needs Work   1   2   3   4   5   Excellent
_____
Paid attention to punctuation

Needs Work   1   2   3   4   5   Excellent
_____
Sounded good

Total Words Read _____

Total Errors − _____

Correct WPM _____

25
Nonfiction

from "Our Miss Brooks:
Gwendolyn Brooks"
by F. Richard Ciccone

Think about the achievement of winning awards usually won
by others.

First Reading

	Words Read	Miscues

Gwendolyn Brooks is a certified part of American literary — 9 _____

history. She was the first black to receive a Pulitzer Prize, winning — 21 _____

in 1950 for her collection *Annie Allen*. — 28 _____

When a *Chicago Tribune* photographer arrived at her house in — 38 _____

1950 after the Pulitzer, Brooks was sitting in the dark, hoping he — 50 _____

would not need to use electricity to take his pictures. She and her — 63 _____

husband, Henry Blakely, had not been able to pay the bill. — 74 _____

When she won her first of three Midwestern Writers poetry — 84 _____

awards, she had not been invited to attend the ceremonies. A few — 96 _____

days later an editor trudged up a long flight of stairs to the — 109 _____

kitchenette apartment at 623 East 63rd Street to deliver the — 119 _____

award. "She said she was shocked to discover I was a Negro." — 131 _____

Two years later, she was in attendance when it was announced — 142 _____

that she had won her third Midwestern Writers award. She sat — 153 _____

still. Finally, Paul Engle, who headed the Creative Writing — 162 _____

Department at the University of Iowa, said, "Gwendolyn, you'd — 171 _____

better come up here or I'll give the prize to someone else." — 183 _____

Brooks recalled, "I'll never forget the gasps that went through — 193 _____

the audience. Remember, things were different then, and Negroes — 202 _____

just didn't win prizes of that sort." — 209 _____

Needs Work   1   2   3   4   5   Excellent
Paid attention to punctuation

Needs Work   1   2   3   4   5   Excellent
Sounded good

Total Words Read _____

Total Errors − _____

Correct WPM _____

from "Our Miss Brooks:
Gwendolyn Brooks"
by F. Richard Ciccone

Think about the achievement of winning awards usually won by others.

	Words Read	Miscues

Gwendolyn Brooks is a certified part of American literary history. She was the first black to receive a Pulitzer Prize, winning in 1950 for her collection *Annie Allen*.

When a *Chicago Tribune* photographer arrived at her house in 1950 after the Pulitzer, Brooks was sitting in the dark, hoping he would not need to use electricity to take his pictures. She and her husband, Henry Blakely, had not been able to pay the bill.

When she won her first of three Midwestern Writers poetry awards, she had not been invited to attend the ceremonies. A few days later an editor trudged up a long flight of stairs to the kitchenette apartment at 623 East 63rd Street to deliver the award. "She said she was shocked to discover I was a Negro."

Two years later, she was in attendance when it was announced that she had won her third Midwestern Writers award. She sat still. Finally, Paul Engle, who headed the Creative Writing Department at the University of Iowa, said, "Gwendolyn, you'd better come up here or I'll give the prize to someone else."

Brooks recalled, "I'll never forget the gasps that went through the audience. Remember, things were different then, and Negroes just didn't win prizes of that sort."

Words Read
9
21
28
38
50
63
74
84
96
109
119
131
142
153
162
171
183
193
202
209

Needs Work   1   2   3   4   5   Excellent
Paid attention to punctuation

Needs Work   1   2   3   4   5   Excellent
Sounded good

Total Words Read _____

Total Errors − _____

Correct WPM _____

26 Becoming a Museum Volunteer

Nonfiction

Learn about the variety of volunteer jobs that are available at a museum.

First Reading

	Words Read	Miscues
Yvonne loved visiting museums and looking at the exhibits.	9	_____
She wanted to work in a museum after she graduated from	20	_____
college, so she consulted museum Web sites on the Internet to	31	_____
find out about the kinds of skills she would need. She soon	43	_____
learned that by volunteering at a museum she could gain	53	_____
experience and learn how a museum operates.	60	_____
Yvonne searched the Web for a nearby museum and was	70	_____
pleased to see that the museum had many volunteer	79	_____
opportunities. She read that she could water plants in the	89	_____
greenhouses or answer phones in an office. She could volunteer	99	_____
at the information desk, greeting visitors and giving them	108	_____
directions. She could volunteer in the public relations department,	117	_____
assembling press packets. Then she saw a volunteer position that	127	_____
fit her interests perfectly. She could work as a docent, giving tours	139	_____
to visitors and telling them about the museum's collection.	148	_____
Without hesitation Yvonne called the museum and asked how	157	_____
to become a docent. She learned that she would first have to	169	_____
complete an application and arrange for an interview. If accepted	179	_____
as a docent, she would then take classes for eight months to learn	192	_____
about the museum's collection. After that she would be ready to	203	_____
give her first tour.	207	_____

Needs Work 1 2 3 4 5 Excellent
Paid attention to punctuation

Needs Work 1 2 3 4 5 Excellent
Sounded good

Total Words Read _____

Total Errors − _____

Correct WPM _____

26 Becoming a Museum Volunteer

Nonfiction

Learn about the variety of volunteer jobs that are available at a museum.

Second Reading

	Words Read	Miscues

Yvonne loved visiting museums and looking at the exhibits. — 9 — _____

She wanted to work in a museum after she graduated from — 20 — _____

college, so she consulted museum Web sites on the Internet to — 31 — _____

find out about the kinds of skills she would need. She soon — 43 — _____

learned that by volunteering at a museum she could gain — 53 — _____

experience and learn how a museum operates. — 60 — _____

Yvonne searched the Web for a nearby museum and was — 70 — _____

pleased to see that the museum had many volunteer — 79 — _____

opportunities. She read that she could water plants in the — 89 — _____

greenhouses or answer phones in an office. She could volunteer — 99 — _____

at the information desk, greeting visitors and giving them — 108 — _____

directions. She could volunteer in the public relations department, — 117 — _____

assembling press packets. Then she saw a volunteer position that — 127 — _____

fit her interests perfectly. She could work as a docent, giving tours — 139 — _____

to visitors and telling them about the museum's collection. — 148 — _____

Without hesitation Yvonne called the museum and asked how — 157 — _____

to become a docent. She learned that she would first have to — 169 — _____

complete an application and arrange for an interview. If accepted — 179 — _____

as a docent, she would then take classes for eight months to learn — 192 — _____

about the museum's collection. After that she would be ready to — 203 — _____

give her first tour. — 207 — _____

Needs Work 1 2 3 4 5 Excellent
Paid attention to punctuation

Needs Work 1 2 3 4 5 Excellent
Sounded good

Total Words Read _____

Total Errors − _____

Correct WPM _____

27 from *The Once and Future King*
Fiction by T. H. White

Take note of Merlyn's remedy for sadness as he instructs the child
who is the future King Arthur.

First Reading

	Words Read	Miscues
"The best thing for being sad," replied Merlyn, beginning to	10	_____
puff and blow, "is to learn something. That is the only thing that	23	_____
never fails. You may grow old and trembling in your anatomies,	34	_____
you may lie awake at night listening to the disorder of your veins,	47	_____
you may miss your only love, you may see the world about you	60	_____
devastated by evil lunatics, or know your honor trampled in the	71	_____
sewers of baser minds. There is only one thing for it then—to	84	_____
learn. Learn why the world wags and what wags it. That is the	97	_____
only thing which the mind can never exhaust, never alienate,	107	_____
never be tortured by, never fear or distrust, and never dream of	119	_____
regretting. Learning is the thing for you. Look at what a lot of	132	_____
things there are to learn—pure science, the only purity there is.	144	_____
You can learn astronomy in a lifetime, natural history in three,	155	_____
literature in six. And then, after you have exhausted a milliard	166	_____
lifetimes in biology and medicine and theocriticism and	174	_____
geography and history and economics—why, you can start to	184	_____
make a cartwheel out of the appropriate wood, or spend fifty	195	_____
years learning to begin to learn to beat your adversary at fencing."	207	_____

Needs Work   1   2   3   4   5   Excellent
_____
          Paid attention to punctuation

Needs Work   1   2   3   4   5   Excellent
_____
          Sounded good

Total Words Read   _____

Total Errors   − _____

Correct WPM   _____

27
Fiction

from *The Once and Future King*
by T. H. White

Take note of Merlyn's remedy for sadness as he instructs the child
who is the future King Arthur.

	Words Read	Miscues

"The best thing for being sad," replied Merlyn, beginning to | 10 | _____ |
puff and blow, "is to learn something. That is the only thing that | 23 | _____ |
never fails. You may grow old and trembling in your anatomies, | 34 | _____ |
you may lie awake at night listening to the disorder of your veins, | 47 | _____ |
you may miss your only love, you may see the world about you | 60 | _____ |
devastated by evil lunatics, or know your honor trampled in the | 71 | _____ |
sewers of baser minds. There is only one thing for it then—to | 84 | _____ |
learn. Learn why the world wags and what wags it. That is the | 97 | _____ |
only thing which the mind can never exhaust, never alienate, | 107 | _____ |
never be tortured by, never fear or distrust, and never dream of | 119 | _____ |
regretting. Learning is the thing for you. Look at what a lot of | 132 | _____ |
things there are to learn—pure science, the only purity there is. | 144 | _____ |
You can learn astronomy in a lifetime, natural history in three, | 155 | _____ |
literature in six. And then, after you have exhausted a milliard | 166 | _____ |
lifetimes in biology and medicine and theocriticism and | 174 | _____ |
geography and history and economics—why, you can start to | 184 | _____ |
make a cartwheel out of the appropriate wood, or spend fifty | 195 | _____ |
years learning to begin to learn to beat your adversary at fencing." | 207 | _____ |

Needs Work   1 2 3 4 5   Excellent
Paid attention to punctuation

Needs Work   1 2 3 4 5   Excellent
Sounded good

Total Words Read _____

Total Errors − _____

Correct WPM _____

28

Fiction

from *Beneath the Wheel*

by Hermann Hesse
translated by Michael Roloff

Consider how the student's unrealistic fear might compare to
similar cares you may have had.

First Reading

	Words Read	Miscues

	Words Read	Miscues
Finally he could think of nothing better to do than recite his	12	_____
irregular verbs but was horrified to discover that he had forgotten	23	_____
practically all of them. He had clean forgotten them! And	33	_____
tomorrow was the examination!	37	_____
His aunt returned, having picked up the news that 118 boys	48	_____
would take the state examination this year and that only 36 could	60	_____
pass. At this point the boy's heart hit absolute rock bottom and he	73	_____
refused to say another word all the way back. At home his	85	_____
headache returned. He refused to eat anything and behaved so	95	_____
strangely that his father gave him a sharp talking to and even his	108	_____
aunt found him impossible. That night he slept deeply but badly,	119	_____
haunted by horrid nightmares: he saw himself sitting in a room	130	_____
with the other 117 candidates; the examiner, who sometimes	139	_____
resembled his pastor at home and then his aunt, kept piling heaps	151	_____
of chocolate in front of him which he was ordered to eat; as he	165	_____
ate, bathed in tears, he saw one candidate after the other get up	178	_____
and leave; they had all eaten their chocolate mountains while his	189	_____
kept growing before his eyes as if it wanted to smother him.	201	_____

Needs Work   1 2 3 4 5   Excellent
Paid attention to punctuation

Needs Work   1 2 3 4 5   Excellent
Sounded good

Total Words Read   _____

Total Errors − _____

Correct WPM   _____

55

from *Beneath the Wheel*

by Hermann Hesse
translated by Michael Roloff

Consider how the student's unrealistic fear might compare to
similar cares you may have had.

	Words Read	Miscues
Finally he could think of nothing better to do than recite his	12	_____
irregular verbs but was horrified to discover that he had forgotten	23	_____
practically all of them. He had clean forgotten them! And	33	_____
tomorrow was the examination!	37	_____
His aunt returned, having picked up the news that 118 boys	48	_____
would take the state examination this year and that only 36 could	60	_____
pass. At this point the boy's heart hit absolute rock bottom and he	73	_____
refused to say another word all the way back. At home his	85	_____
headache returned. He refused to eat anything and behaved so	95	_____
strangely that his father gave him a sharp talking to and even his	108	_____
aunt found him impossible. That night he slept deeply but badly,	119	_____
haunted by horrid nightmares: he saw himself sitting in a room	130	_____
with the other 117 candidates; the examiner, who sometimes	139	_____
resembled his pastor at home and then his aunt, kept piling heaps	151	_____
of chocolate in front of him which he was ordered to eat; as he	165	_____
ate, bathed in tears, he saw one candidate after the other get up	178	_____
and leave; they had all eaten their chocolate mountains while his	189	_____
kept growing before his eyes as if it wanted to smother him.	201	_____

Needs Work   1 2 3 4 5   Excellent
Paid attention to punctuation

Needs Work   1 2 3 4 5   Excellent
Sounded good

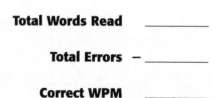

Total Words Read _____

Total Errors − _____

Correct WPM _____

29 from *1984*

Fiction by George Orwell

Note how the author makes the character feel the transition from
a dream to conscious reality.

First Reading

	Words Read	Miscues
He could not remember what had happened, but he knew	10	_____
in his dream that in some way the lives of his mother and his	24	_____
sister had been sacrificed to his own. It was one of those dreams	37	_____
which, while retaining the characteristic dream scenery, [is] a	46	_____
continuation of one's intellectual life, and in which one becomes	56	_____
aware of facts and ideas which still seem new and valuable after	68	_____
one is awake. The thing that now suddenly struck Winston was	79	_____
that his mother's death, nearly thirty years ago, had been tragic	90	_____
and sorrowful in a way that was no longer possible. Tragedy, he	102	_____
perceived, belonged to the ancient time, to a time when there	113	_____
were still privacy, love, and friendship, and when the members of	124	_____
a family stood by one another without needing to know the	135	_____
reason. His mother's memory tore at his heart because she had	146	_____
died loving him, when he was too young and selfish to love her in	160	_____
return, and because somehow, he did not remember how, she had	171	_____
sacrificed herself to a conception of loyalty that was private and	182	_____
unalterable. Such things, he saw, could not happen today. Today	192	_____
there were fear, hatred, and pain, but no dignity of emotion, or	204	_____
deep or complex sorrows.	208	_____

Needs Work 1 2 3 4 5 Excellent
Paid attention to punctuation

Needs Work 1 2 3 4 5 Excellent
Sounded good

Total Words Read _____

Total Errors − _____

Correct WPM _____

29

Fiction

from *1984*

by George Orwell

Note how the author makes the character feel the transition from
a dream to conscious reality.

	Words Read	Miscues

He could not remember what had happened, but he knew
in his dream that in some way the lives of his mother and his
sister had been sacrificed to his own. It was one of those dreams
which, while retaining the characteristic dream scenery, [is] a
continuation of one's intellectual life, and in which one becomes
aware of facts and ideas which still seem new and valuable after
one is awake. The thing that now suddenly struck Winston was
that his mother's death, nearly thirty years ago, had been tragic
and sorrowful in a way that was no longer possible. Tragedy, he
perceived, belonged to the ancient time, to a time when there
were still privacy, love, and friendship, and when the members of
a family stood by one another without needing to know the
reason. His mother's memory tore at his heart because she had
died loving him, when he was too young and selfish to love her in
return, and because somehow, he did not remember how, she had
sacrificed herself to a conception of loyalty that was private and
unalterable. Such things, he saw, could not happen today. Today
there were fear, hatred, and pain, but no dignity of emotion, or
deep or complex sorrows.

Words Read
10
24
37
46
56
68
79
90
102
113
124
135
146
160
171
182
192
204
208

Needs Work   1   2   3   4   5   Excellent
Paid attention to punctuation

Needs Work   1   2   3   4   5   Excellent
Sounded good

Total Words Read _____

Total Errors − _____

Correct WPM _____

30
Nonfiction

from *Black Ice*
by Lorene Cary

Travel with the narrator as she revisits the neighborhood of her youth.

First Reading

	Words Read	Miscues

My father steered us through Germantown, where wet leaves lay | 10 | _____
in treacherous layers over trolley tracks and cobblestones. Cars | 19 | _____
slipped on and off the rails and then swerved to avoid each other, | 32 | _____
making rubbery squeals and muffled thuds. | 38 | _____

By the time we pulled into the stone driveway, I felt as if we | 52 | _____
were a long way away from our home in the west end of Yeadon, | 66 | _____
an enclave of black professionals, paraprofessionals, wish-they- | 74 | _____
was-, look-like-, and might-as-well-be professionals, as we called | 86 | _____
ourselves. We were far away from the black suburb that, as a West | 99 | _____
Philly transplant, I disliked for its self-satisfied smugness. When | 108 | _____
we'd moved from our city apartment—from the living room with | 119 | _____
a convertible couch where my parents slept, from the bedroom | 129 | _____
where my sister and I slept (which was transformed into a dining | 141 | _____
room at Christmas), and from the kitchen where we normally ate, | 152 | _____
and where my mother pressed and curled women's hair in the | 163 | _____
evenings—Yeadon had impressed me with its leafy green | 172 | _____
grandeur and insularity. But now, as we stood in the Chestnut Hill | 184 | _____
driveway, I saw how modest our Tudors were, our semidetached | 194 | _____
Dutch colonials, our muddy driveways and the cyclone fences that | 204 | _____
held in our dogs. | 208 | _____

Needs Work   1 2 3 4 5   Excellent
    Paid attention to punctuation

Needs Work   1 2 3 4 5   Excellent
    Sounded good

Total Words Read   _____

Total Errors − _____

Correct WPM   _____

from *Black Ice*

by Lorene Cary

Travel with the narrator as she revisits the neighborhood of her youth.

	Words Read	Miscues
My father steered us through Germantown, where wet leaves lay	10	_____
in treacherous layers over trolley tracks and cobblestones. Cars	19	_____
slipped on and off the rails and then swerved to avoid each other,	32	_____
making rubbery squeals and muffled thuds.	38	_____
By the time we pulled into the stone driveway, I felt as if we	52	_____
were a long way away from our home in the west end of Yeadon,	66	_____
an enclave of black professionals, paraprofessionals, wish-they-	74	_____
was-, look-like-, and might-as-well-be professionals, as we called	86	_____
ourselves. We were far away from the black suburb that, as a West	99	_____
Philly transplant, I disliked for its self-satisfied smugness. When	108	_____
we'd moved from our city apartment—from the living room with	119	_____
a convertible couch where my parents slept, from the bedroom	129	_____
where my sister and I slept (which was transformed into a dining	141	_____
room at Christmas), and from the kitchen where we normally ate,	152	_____
and where my mother pressed and curled women's hair in the	163	_____
evenings—Yeadon had impressed me with its leafy green	172	_____
grandeur and insularity. But now, as we stood in the Chestnut Hill	184	_____
driveway, I saw how modest our Tudors were, our semidetached	194	_____
Dutch colonials, our muddy driveways and the cyclone fences that	204	_____
held in our dogs.	208	_____

Needs Work   1   2   3   4   5   Excellent
Paid attention to punctuation

Needs Work   1   2   3   4   5   Excellent
Sounded good

Total Words Read   _____

Total Errors   − _____

Correct WPM   _____

31

Fiction

from *A Separate Peace*
by John Knowles

Picture the surroundings of Devon School in this passage from John Knowles's classic novel.

First Reading

	Words Read	Miscues

Devon is sometimes considered the most beautiful school in | 9 | _____
New England, and even on this dismal afternoon its power was | 20 | _____
asserted. It is the beauty of small areas of order—a large yard, a | 34 | _____
group of trees, three similar dormitories, a circle of old houses— | 45 | _____
living together in contentious harmony. You felt that an argument | 55 | _____
might begin again any time; in fact it had: out of the Dean's | 68 | _____
Residence, a pure and authentic Colonial house, there now | 77 | _____
sprouted an ell with a big bare picture window. Some day the | 89 | _____
Dean would probably live entirely encased in a house of glass and | 101 | _____
be happy as a sandpiper. Everything at Devon slowly changed and | 112 | _____
slowly harmonized with what had gone before. So it was logical to | 124 | _____
hope that since the buildings and the Deans and the curriculum | 135 | _____
could achieve this, I could achieve, perhaps unknowingly already | 144 | _____
had achieved, this growth and harmony myself. | 151 | _____

I would know more about that when I had seen the second | 163 | _____
place I had come to see. So I roamed on past the balanced red | 177 | _____
brick dormitories with webs of leafless ivy clinging to them, | 187 | _____
through a ramshackle salient of the town which invaded the | 197 | _____
school for a hundred yards, past the solid gymnasium, full of | 208 | _____
students at this hour but silent as a monument on the outside. | 220 | _____

Needs Work   1 2 3 4 5   Excellent
Paid attention to punctuation

Needs Work   1 2 3 4 5   Excellent
Sounded good

Total Words Read _____

Total Errors − _____

Correct WPM _____

31

Fiction

from *A Separate Peace*

by John Knowles

Picture the surroundings of Devon School in this passage from
John Knowles's classic novel.

	Words Read	Miscues

Devon is sometimes considered the most beautiful school in
New England, and even on this dismal afternoon its power was
asserted. It is the beauty of small areas of order—a large yard, a
group of trees, three similar dormitories, a circle of old houses—
living together in contentious harmony. You felt that an argument
might begin again any time; in fact it had: out of the Dean's
Residence, a pure and authentic Colonial house, there now
sprouted an ell with a big bare picture window. Some day the
Dean would probably live entirely encased in a house of glass and
be happy as a sandpiper. Everything at Devon slowly changed and
slowly harmonized with what had gone before. So it was logical to
hope that since the buildings and the Deans and the curriculum
could achieve this, I could achieve, perhaps unknowingly already
had achieved, this growth and harmony myself.

I would know more about that when I had seen the second
place I had come to see. So I roamed on past the balanced red
brick dormitories with webs of leafless ivy clinging to them,
through a ramshackle salient of the town which invaded the
school for a hundred yards, past the solid gymnasium, full of
students at this hour but silent as a monument on the outside.

Words Read
9
20
34
45
55
68
77
89
101
112
124
135
144
151
163
177
187
197
208
220

Needs Work   1   2   3   4   5   Excellent
    Paid attention to punctuation

Needs Work   1   2   3   4   5   Excellent
    Sounded good

Total Words Read _____

Total Errors − _____

Correct WPM _____

The Lasting Impact of Jan Ernst Matzeliger

Nonfiction

Meet the man who revolutionized the shoe industry.

First Reading

	Words Read	Miscues

Jan Ernst Matzeliger came to the United States from South   10   _____

America in the 1870s. As a child, Matzeliger had a talent for   22   _____

repairing machinery. As an adult, he invented a device that   32   _____

revolutionized the shoe industry.   36   _____

In the late 1870s, Matzeliger worked for a shoe manufacturer.   46   _____

At that time, machines cut and stitched the upper part of a shoe,   59   _____

but workers called hand lasters attached the uppers to the soles   70   _____

manually. Skilled hand lasters could produce 50 pairs of shoes in   81   _____

10 hours and commanded high wages for their work. Even so,   92   _____

they could not assemble a shoe so quickly as machines could   103   _____

produce its parts.   106   _____

Many people believed that no one could invent a machine   116   _____

to do the hand lasters' work, but Matzeliger disagreed. For years   127   _____

he labored to develop a lasting machine. He used his knowledge   138   _____

of shoemaking and his ingenuity to develop models. At first   148   _____

Matzeliger used remnants of wood, scrap metal, and other   157   _____

discarded materials to make his models. Instead of buying   166   _____

food, he spent his earnings to purchase better materials for his   177   _____

lasting machine.   179   _____

Finally, Matzeliger's lasting machine was ready. In one day, it   189   _____

could assemble more than 10 times as many shoes as a person   201   _____

could and could produce shoes more cheaply. As a result, more   212   _____

people could afford to wear shoes.   218   _____

Needs Work   1   2   3   4   5   Excellent
     Paid attention to punctuation

Needs Work   1   2   3   4   5   Excellent
     Sounded good

Total Words Read   _____

Total Errors   − _____

Correct WPM   _____

The Lasting Impact of Jan Ernst Matzeliger

Meet the man who revolutionized the shoe industry.

	Words Read	Miscues
Jan Ernst Matzeliger came to the United States from South	10	_____
America in the 1870s. As a child, Matzeliger had a talent for	22	_____
repairing machinery. As an adult, he invented a device that	32	_____
revolutionized the shoe industry.	36	_____
In the late 1870s, Matzeliger worked for a shoe manufacturer.	46	_____
At that time, machines cut and stitched the upper part of a shoe,	59	_____
but workers called hand lasters attached the uppers to the soles	70	_____
manually. Skilled hand lasters could produce 50 pairs of shoes in	81	_____
10 hours and commanded high wages for their work. Even so,	92	_____
they could not assemble a shoe so quickly as machines could	103	_____
produce its parts.	106	_____
Many people believed that no one could invent a machine	116	_____
to do the hand lasters' work, but Matzeliger disagreed. For years	127	_____
he labored to develop a lasting machine. He used his knowledge	138	_____
of shoemaking and his ingenuity to develop models. At first	148	_____
Matzeliger used remnants of wood, scrap metal, and other	157	_____
discarded materials to make his models. Instead of buying	166	_____
food, he spent his earnings to purchase better materials for	177	_____
his lasting machine.	179	_____
Finally, Matzeliger's lasting machine was ready. In one day, it	189	_____
could assemble more than 10 times as many shoes as a person	201	_____
could and could produce shoes more cheaply. As a result, more	212	_____
people could afford to wear shoes.	218	_____

Needs Work   1   2   3   4   5   Excellent
Paid attention to punctuation

Needs Work   1   2   3   4   5   Excellent
Sounded good

Total Words Read _____

Total Errors − _____

Correct WPM _____

33

Fiction

from *Lord Jim*
by Joseph Conrad

Think about the capability of the chief mate as he recalls the
power of the angry sea.

First Reading

	Words Read	Miscues

	Words Read	Miscues
He was gentlemanly, steady, with a thorough knowledge of his	10	_____
duties; and in time, when yet very young, he became chief mate of	23	_____
a fine ship, without ever having been tested by those events of the	36	_____
sea that show in the light of day the inner worth of a man, the	51	_____
edge of his temper, and the fiber of his stuff; that reveal the	64	_____
quality of his resistance and the secret truth of his pretences, not	76	_____
only to others but also to himself.	83	_____
Only once in all that time he had again the glimpse of the	96	_____
earnestness in the anger of the sea. That truth is not so often	109	_____
made apparent as people might think. There are many shades in	120	_____
the danger of adventures and gales, and it is only now and then	133	_____
that there appears on the face of facts a sinister violence of	145	_____
intention—that indefinable something which forces it upon the	154	_____
mind and the heart of a man, that this complication of accidents	166	_____
or these elemental furies are coming at him with a purpose of	178	_____
malice, with a strength beyond control, with an unbridled cruelty	188	_____
that means to tear out of him his hope and his fear, the pain of	203	_____
his fatigue and his longing for rest.	210	_____

Needs Work   1 2 3 4 5   Excellent
_____
Paid attention to punctuation

Needs Work   1 2 3 4 5   Excellent
_____
Sounded good

Total Words Read _____

Total Errors – _____

Correct WPM _____

33

Fiction

from *Lord Jim*

by Joseph Conrad

Think about the capability of the chief mate as he recalls the power of the angry sea.

	Words Read	Miscues
He was gentlemanly, steady, with a thorough knowledge of his	10	_____
duties; and in time, when yet very young, he became chief mate of	23	_____
a fine ship, without ever having been tested by those events of the	36	_____
sea that show in the light of day the inner worth of a man, the	51	_____
edge of his temper, and the fiber of his stuff; that reveal the	64	_____
quality of his resistance and the secret truth of his pretences, not	76	_____
only to others but also to himself.	83	_____
Only once in all that time he had again the glimpse of the	96	_____
earnestness in the anger of the sea. That truth is not so often	109	_____
made apparent as people might think. There are many shades in	120	_____
the danger of adventures and gales, and it is only now and then	133	_____
that there appears on the face of facts a sinister violence of	145	_____
intention—that indefinable something which forces it upon the	154	_____
mind and the heart of a man, that this complication of accidents	166	_____
or these elemental furies are coming at him with a purpose of	178	_____
malice, with a strength beyond control, with an unbridled cruelty	188	_____
that means to tear out of him his hope and his fear, the pain of	203	_____
his fatigue and his longing for rest.	210	_____

Needs Work   1 2 3 4 5   Excellent
Paid attention to punctuation

Needs Work   1 2 3 4 5   Excellent
Sounded good

Total Words Read _____

Total Errors − _____

Correct WPM _____

34

Nonfiction

The Stock Market Crash of 1929

First Reading

Take a look at the events surrounding the financial panic that sparked the Great Depression.

	Words Read	Miscues
As the 1920s progressed, American businesses were thriving	8	_____
and the economy booming. Many people were investing money in	18	_____
the stock market and buying shares of stock.	26	_____
Between 1925 and 1929, the value of most stocks more than	37	_____
doubled. Investors who sold their shares when the price increased	47	_____
made a great deal of money. This led numerous speculators to	58	_____
borrow money to invest in the stock market. They planned to sell	70	_____
their shares when the stock increased in value. However, this	80	_____
injection of money into the market inflated stock prices beyond	90	_____
the worth of the stocks. On October 24, 1929, the surge in stock	103	_____
prices turned into a plunge. By October 29, stock prices had	114	_____
decreased even further, causing numerous investors to panic and	123	_____
sell their stocks, even though the stocks were worth less than their	135	_____
purchase price.	137	_____
By the end of the year, investors had lost billions in the stock	150	_____
market crash. Banks and businesses that had lost heavily in the	161	_____
stock market closed. Millions of people lost their savings when	171	_____
banks failed. As banks and businesses closed, the people they	181	_____
employed lost their jobs. The stock market crash of 1929	191	_____
contributed to the decline of the American economy and the	201	_____
resulting Great Depression, which would last into the 1940s in	211	_____
the United States.	214	_____

Needs Work   1   2   3   4   5   Excellent
Paid attention to punctuation

Needs Work   1   2   3   4   5   Excellent
Sounded good

Total Words Read   _____

Total Errors   − _____

Correct WPM   _____

The Stock Market Crash of 1929

Take a look at the events surrounding the financial panic that sparked the Great Depression.

	Words Read	Miscues
As the 1920s progressed, American businesses were thriving	8	_____
and the economy booming. Many people were investing money in	18	_____
the stock market and buying shares of stock.	26	_____
Between 1925 and 1929, the value of most stocks more than	37	_____
doubled. Investors who sold their shares when the price increased	47	_____
made a great deal of money. This led numerous speculators to	58	_____
borrow money to invest in the stock market. They planned to sell	70	_____
their shares when the stock increased in value. However, this	80	_____
injection of money into the market inflated stock prices beyond	90	_____
the worth of the stocks. On October 24, 1929, the surge in stock	103	_____
prices turned into a plunge. By October 29, stock prices had	114	_____
decreased even further, causing numerous investors to panic and	123	_____
sell their stocks, even though the stocks were worth less than their	135	_____
purchase price.	137	_____
By the end of the year, investors had lost billions in the stock	150	_____
market crash. Banks and businesses that had lost heavily in the	161	_____
stock market closed. Millions of people lost their savings when	171	_____
banks failed. As banks and businesses closed, the people they	181	_____
employed lost their jobs. The stock market crash of 1929	191	_____
contributed to the decline of the American economy and the	201	_____
resulting Great Depression, which would last into the 1940s in	211	_____
the United States.	214	_____

Needs Work   1 2 3 4 5   Excellent

Paid attention to punctuation

Needs Work   1 2 3 4 5   Excellent

Sounded good

Total Words Read   _____

Total Errors − _____

Correct WPM   _____

35 Boston's MBTA

Nonfiction

Track the development of this country's oldest system of public transportation.

	Words Read	Miscues
The Massachusetts Bay Transportation Authority (MBTA) runs	7	_____
the oldest system of public transportation in the United States.	17	_____
It had its beginnings in 1631, when the government of the	28	_____
Massachusetts Bay Colony allowed Thomas Williams to run a	37	_____
ferry between Chelsea and Boston. This service changed a two-day	47	_____
ride over land into a three-mile trip across Boston Harbor.	57	_____
Travelers relied on ferries for another hundred years until bridges	67	_____
were built across the harbor and the Charles River.	76	_____
It became a great deal easier to get from place to place	88	_____
in Boston during the 1800s. The Omnibus was the first	98	_____
improvement. This horse-drawn wagon was lined with benches,	106	_____
and passengers could get on or off at various points along	117	_____
a set route. Later on, trolleys on railway tracks carried people	128	_____
throughout the city and into nearby towns. On New Year's Day	139	_____
in 1889, the first electric trolley was put into service. The first	151	_____
subway, or underground train, opened in Boston in 1897.	160	_____
Since 1964 the U.S. Department of Transportation has	168	_____
helped the MBTA grow. Economic problems, rising fuel costs,	177	_____
population growth, and concerns about air pollution in the	186	_____
1970s have tested the MBTA's capacities. However, today the MBTA	196	_____
has trains, buses, and boats that serve 175 cities and cover more	208	_____
than 3,000 square miles in eastern Massachusetts.	215	_____

Needs Work   1 2 3 4 5   Excellent
Paid attention to punctuation

Needs Work   1 2 3 4 5   Excellent
Sounded good

Total Words Read _____

Total Errors − _____

Correct WPM _____

Boston's MBTA

Track the development of this country's oldest system of public transportation.

	Words Read	Miscues
The Massachusetts Bay Transportation Authority (MBTA) runs	7	_____
the oldest system of public transportation in the United States.	17	_____
It had its beginnings in 1631, when the government of the	28	_____
Massachusetts Bay Colony allowed Thomas Williams to run a	37	_____
ferry between Chelsea and Boston. This service changed a two-day	47	_____
ride over land into a three-mile trip across Boston Harbor.	57	_____
Travelers relied on ferries for another hundred years until bridges	67	_____
were built across the harbor and the Charles River.	76	_____
It became a great deal easier to get from place to place	88	_____
in Boston during the 1800s. The Omnibus was the first	98	_____
improvement. This horse-drawn wagon was lined with benches,	106	_____
and passengers could get on or off at various points along	117	_____
a set route. Later on, trolleys on railway tracks carried people	128	_____
throughout the city and into nearby towns. On New Year's Day	139	_____
in 1889, the first electric trolley was put into service. The first	151	_____
subway, or underground train, opened in Boston in 1897.	160	_____
Since 1964 the U.S. Department of Transportation has	168	_____
helped the MBTA grow. Economic problems, rising fuel costs,	177	_____
population growth, and concerns about air pollution in the	186	_____
1970s have tested the MBTA's capacities. However, today the MBTA	196	_____
has trains, buses, and boats that serve 175 cities and cover more	208	_____
than 3,000 square miles in eastern Massachusetts.	215	_____

Needs Work   1   2   3   4   5   Excellent
Paid attention to punctuation

Needs Work   1   2   3   4   5   Excellent
Sounded good

Total Words Read   _____

Total Errors − _____

Correct WPM   _____

36
Nonfiction

Oliver Wendell Holmes Jr.:
Supreme Court Justice

First Reading

Become acquainted with the most famous Supreme Court justice in U.S. history.

	Words Read	Miscues

Oliver Wendell Holmes Jr. was born in Boston, Massachusetts, — 9 — _____
in 1841. Named for his father, a great writer, Holmes possessed a — 21 — _____
similar talent for writing. As a young man, he attended Harvard — 32 — _____
College—writing essays for, and later becoming editor of, the — 42 — _____
Harvard Magazine. Following his graduation, Holmes sustained — 49 — _____
several injuries on the battlefield for the Union Army in the Civil — 61 — _____
War. After three years of war service, he returned to Harvard Law — 73 — _____
School to study law and become an attorney. — 81 — _____

Holmes began his career as a lawyer in Boston in 1867. — 92 — _____
Aside from his duties as an attorney, Holmes lectured on the — 103 — _____
fundamentals of American law. He also wrote about the subject in — 114 — _____
a renowned work titled *The Common Law.* After the publication — 124 — _____
of his book, Holmes taught at Harvard for a term before being — 136 — _____
appointed to the Massachusetts Supreme Court. — 142 — _____

In 1902 Holmes became a justice of the U.S. Supreme Court. — 153 — _____
Known as the "great dissenter," he often disagreed with the other — 164 — _____
justices. Holmes frequently wrote his opinions of the law, in — 174 — _____
defense of such rights as freedom of speech and that of workers — 186 — _____
to form unions. — 189 — _____

Health problems forced Holmes to retire from the Supreme — 198 — _____
Court in 1932 after serving for 30 years. He died three years later — 211 — _____
at the age of 93. — 216 — _____

Needs Work   1 2 3 4 5   Excellent
Paid attention to punctuation

Needs Work   1 2 3 4 5   Excellent
Sounded good

Total Words Read _____

Total Errors − _____

Correct WPM _____

36 Oliver Wendell Holmes Jr.:

Nonfiction

Supreme Court Justice

Become acquainted with the most famous Supreme Court justice in U.S. history.

Second Reading

	Words Read	Miscues
Oliver Wendell Holmes Jr. was born in Boston, Massachusetts,	9	_____
in 1841. Named for his father, a great writer, Holmes possessed a	21	_____
similar talent for writing. As a young man, he attended Harvard	32	_____
College—writing essays for, and later becoming editor of, the	42	_____
Harvard Magazine. Following his graduation, Holmes sustained	49	_____
several injuries on the battlefield for the Union Army in the Civil	61	_____
War. After three years of war service, he returned to Harvard Law	73	_____
School to study law and become an attorney.	81	_____
Holmes began his career as a lawyer in Boston in 1867.	92	_____
Aside from his duties as an attorney, Holmes lectured on the	103	_____
fundamentals of American law. He also wrote about the subject in	114	_____
a renowned work titled *The Common Law*. After the publication	124	_____
of his book, Holmes taught at Harvard for a term before being	136	_____
appointed to the Massachusetts Supreme Court.	142	_____
In 1902 Holmes became a justice of the U.S. Supreme Court.	153	_____
Known as the "great dissenter," he often disagreed with the other	164	_____
justices. Holmes frequently wrote his opinions of the law, in	174	_____
defense of such rights as freedom of speech and that of workers	186	_____
to form unions.	189	_____
Health problems forced Holmes to retire from the Supreme	198	_____
Court in 1932 after serving for 30 years. He died three years later	211	_____
at the age of 93.	216	_____

Needs Work   1 2 3 4 5   Excellent
           Paid attention to punctuation

Needs Work   1 2 3 4 5   Excellent
              Sounded good

Total Words Read   _____

Total Errors – _____

Correct WPM   _____

37

Fiction

from ***The Red Badge of Courage***

by Stephen Crane

Feel the heat of the Civil War as you read this excerpt from an American classic.

First Reading

	Words Read	Miscues

During the battle there was a singular absence of heroic poses. — 11 — _____

The men bending and surging in their haste and rage were in — 23 — _____

every impossible attitude. The steel ramrods clanked and clanged — 32 — _____

with incessant din as the men pounded them furiously into the — 43 — _____

hot rifle barrels. The flaps of the cartridge boxes were all — 54 — _____

unfastened and bobbed idiotically with each movement. The — 62 — _____

rifles, once loaded, were jerked to the shoulder and fired without — 73 — _____

apparent aim into the smoke or at one of the blurred and shifting — 86 — _____

forms which, upon the field before the regiment, had been — 96 — _____

growing larger and larger like puppets under a magician's hand. — 106 — _____

　　The officers, at their intervals, rearward, neglected to stand in — 116 — _____

picturesque attitudes. They were bobbing to and fro, roaring — 125 — _____

directions and encouragements. The dimensions of their howls — 133 — _____

were extraordinary. And often they nearly stood upon their heads — 143 — _____

in their anxiety to observe the enemy on the other side of the — 156 — _____

tumbling smoke. — 158 — _____

　　The lieutenant of the youth's company had encountered a — 167 — _____

soldier who had fled screaming at the first volley of his comrades. — 179 — _____

The man was blubbering and staring with sheeplike eyes at the — 190 — _____

lieutenant, who had seized him by the collar and drove him back — 202 — _____

into the ranks. — 205 — _____

Needs Work　1　2　3　4　5　Excellent
Paid attention to punctuation

Needs Work　1　2　3　4　5　Excellent
Sounded good

Total Words Read　_____

Total Errors − _____

Correct WPM　_____

37

Fiction

from *The Red Badge of Courage*

by Stephen Crane

Feel the heat of the Civil War as you read this excerpt from an American classic.

	Words Read	Miscues
During the battle there was a singular absence of heroic poses.	11	_____
The men bending and surging in their haste and rage were in	23	_____
every impossible attitude. The steel ramrods clanked and clanged	32	_____
with incessant din as the men pounded them furiously into the	43	_____
hot rifle barrels. The flaps of the cartridge boxes were all	54	_____
unfastened and bobbed idiotically with each movement. The	62	_____
rifles, once loaded, were jerked to the shoulder and fired without	73	_____
apparent aim into the smoke or at one of the blurred and shifting	86	_____
forms which, upon the field before the regiment, had been	96	_____
growing larger and larger like puppets under a magician's hand.	106	_____
The officers, at their intervals, rearward, neglected to stand in	116	_____
picturesque attitudes. They were bobbing to and fro, roaring	125	_____
directions and encouragements. The dimensions of their howls	133	_____
were extraordinary. And often they nearly stood upon their heads	143	_____
in their anxiety to observe the enemy on the other side of the	156	_____
tumbling smoke.	158	_____
The lieutenant of the youth's company had encountered a	167	_____
soldier who had fled screaming at the first volley of his comrades.	179	_____
The man was blubbering and staring with sheeplike eyes at the	190	_____
lieutenant, who had seized him by the collar and drove him back	202	_____
into the ranks.	205	_____

Needs Work 1 2 3 4 5 Excellent

Paid attention to punctuation

Needs Work 1 2 3 4 5 Excellent

Sounded good

Total Words Read _____

Total Errors − _____

Correct WPM _____

38

Nonfiction

from "Does Homer Have Legs?"
by David Denby

Follow along as the author recalls a favorite college memory—
selecting books at the campus bookstore.

First Reading

	Words Read	Miscues
The required books for each course were laid out on shelves in	12	_____
the college bookstore, and I would stare at them a long time,	24	_____
lifting them, turning the pages, pretending I didn't really *need* this	35	_____
one or that, laying it down and then picking it up again. If no one	50	_____
was looking, I would even smell a few of them and feel the	63	_____
pages—I had a thing about books as physical objects, and I was	76	_____
happy when I discovered that Edmund Wilson, my idol, also had	87	_____
strong feelings about the feel and size of a book.	97	_____
It wasn't just reading that excited me but the *idea* of reading	109	_____
the big books, the promise of enlargement, the adventure of	119	_____
strangeness. The love of reading has within it a collector's passion,	130	_____
the desire to possess: I would swallow the whole store. Reality	141	_____
never entered into this. The difficulty or the tedium of the books,	153	_____
the droning performance of the teacher, the blanking out of my	164	_____
own attention in a post-midterm swoon—none of this mattered	174	_____
at the moment of anticipation, which was renewed each term. I	185	_____
might have spent most of the previous semester in a self-absorbed	196	_____
funk, but I roused myself at the beginning of the new semester for	209	_____
the wonderful ritual of the bookstore.	215	_____

Needs Work   1 2 3 4 5   Excellent
Paid attention to punctuation

Needs Work   1 2 3 4 5   Excellent
Sounded good

Total Words Read   _____

Total Errors   − _____

Correct WPM   _____

from **"Does Homer Have Legs?"**

by David Denby

Follow along as the author recalls a favorite college memory—
selecting books at the campus bookstore.

The required books for each course were laid out on shelves in	12	_____
the college bookstore, and I would stare at them a long time,	24	_____
lifting them, turning the pages, pretending I didn't really *need* this	35	_____
one or that, laying it down and then picking it up again. If no one	50	_____
was looking, I would even smell a few of them and feel the	63	_____
pages—I had a thing about books as physical objects, and I was	76	_____
happy when I discovered that Edmund Wilson, my idol, also had	87	_____
strong feelings about the feel and size of a book.	97	_____
It wasn't just reading that excited me but the *idea* of reading	109	_____
the big books, the promise of enlargement, the adventure of	119	_____
strangeness. The love of reading has within it a collector's passion,	130	_____
the desire to possess: I would swallow the whole store. Reality	141	_____
never entered into this. The difficulty or the tedium of the books,	153	_____
the droning performance of the teacher, the blanking out of my	164	_____
own attention in a post-midterm swoon—none of this mattered	174	_____
at the moment of anticipation, which was renewed each term. I	185	_____
might have spent most of the previous semester in a self-absorbed	196	_____
funk, but I roused myself at the beginning of the new semester for	209	_____
the wonderful ritual of the bookstore.	215	_____

Needs Work   1   2   3   4   5   Excellent
Paid attention to punctuation

Needs Work   1   2   3   4   5   Excellent
Sounded good

Total Words Read   _____

Total Errors   – _____

Correct WPM   _____

39 from *Love Medicine*

Fiction   by Louise Erdrich

Walk with this salesman and learn his techniques for selling door to door.

First Reading

	Words Read	Miscues

Door to door, [Bev had] sold children's after-school home workbooks for the past eighteen years. The wonder of it was that he had sold any workbook sets at all, for he was not an educated man and if the customers had, as they might naturally do, considered him an example of his product's efficiency they might not have entrusted their own children to those pages of sums and reading exercises. But they did buy the workbook sets regularly, for Bev's ploy was to use his humble appearance and faulty grammar to ease into conversation with his hardworking, get-ahead customers. They looked forward to seeing the higher qualities, which they could not afford, inculcated in their own children. [Bev's] territory was a small-town world of earnest dreamers. Part of Bev's pitch, and the one that usually sold the books, was to show the wife or husband a wallet-sized school photo of his son.

That was Henry Junior. The back of the photo was inscribed "To Uncle Hat," but the customer never saw that, because the precious relic was encased in a cardboard-backed sheet of clear plastic. This covering preserved it from thousands of mill-toughened thumbs in the working-class sections of Minneapolis and small towns within its one-hundred-mile radius.

Words Read	Miscues
9	_____
21	_____
35	_____
46	_____
56	_____
67	_____
77	_____
88	_____
97	_____
106	_____
116	_____
125	_____
137	_____
148	_____
152	_____
163	_____
174	_____
184	_____
193	_____
202	_____
207	_____

Needs Work   1   2   3   4   5   Excellent
Paid attention to punctuation

Needs Work   1   2   3   4   5   Excellent
Sounded good

Total Words Read _____

Total Errors − _____

Correct WPM _____

39

Fiction

from *Love Medicine*

by Louise Erdrich

Walk with this salesman and learn his techniques for selling door to door.

	Words Read	Miscues

Door to door, [Bev had] sold children's after-school home workbooks for the past eighteen years. The wonder of it was that he had sold any workbook sets at all, for he was not an educated man and if the customers had, as they might naturally do, considered him an example of his product's efficiency they might not have entrusted their own children to those pages of sums and reading exercises. But they did buy the workbook sets regularly, for Bev's ploy was to use his humble appearance and faulty grammar to ease into conversation with his hardworking, get-ahead customers. They looked forward to seeing the higher qualities, which they could not afford, inculcated in their own children. [Bev's] territory was a small-town world of earnest dreamers. Part of Bev's pitch, and the one that usually sold the books, was to show the wife or husband a wallet-sized school photo of his son.

That was Henry Junior. The back of the photo was inscribed "To Uncle Hat," but the customer never saw that, because the precious relic was encased in a cardboard-backed sheet of clear plastic. This covering preserved it from thousands of mill-toughened thumbs in the working-class sections of Minneapolis and small towns within its one-hundred-mile radius.

Words Read
9
21
35
46
56
67
77
88
97
106
116
125
137
148
152
163
174
184
193
202
207

Needs Work   1   2   3   4   5   Excellent

Paid attention to punctuation

Needs Work   1   2   3   4   5   Excellent

Sounded good

Total Words Read _____

Total Errors − _____

Correct WPM _____

40

Nonfiction

from *The Ledge Between the Streams*
by Ved Mehta

Learn about the Hindu tradition of arranged marriages.

	Words Read	Miscues
[Father] started talking as if we were all very small and he were	13	_____
conducting one of our "dinner-table-school" discussions. He	20	_____
said that by right and tradition the oldest daughter had to be	32	_____
given in marriage first, and that the ripe age for marriage was	44	_____
nineteen. He said that when a girl approached that age her	55	_____
parents, who had to take the initiative, made many inquiries and	66	_____
followed many leads. They investigated each young man and his	76	_____
family background, his relatives, his friends, his classmates,	84	_____
because it was important to know what kind of family the girl	96	_____
would be marrying into, what kind of company she would be	107	_____
expected to keep. If the girl's parents decided that a particular	118	_____
young man was suitable, then his people also had to make their	130	_____
investigations, but, however favorable their findings, their decision	138	_____
was unpredictable, because good, well-settled boys were in great	147	_____
demand and could afford to be choosy. All this took a lot of time.	161	_____
"That's why I said nothing to you children about why I went to	174	_____
Mussoorie," he concluded. "I went to see a young man for Pom.	186	_____
She's already nineteen."	189	_____
We were stunned. We have never really faced the idea that	200	_____
Sister Pom might get married and suddenly leave, I thought.	210	_____

Needs Work   1 2 3 4 5   Excellent
Paid attention to punctuation

Needs Work   1 2 3 4 5   Excellent
Sounded good

Total Words Read _____

Total Errors − _____

Correct WPM _____

from *The Ledge Between the Streams*
by Ved Mehta

Learn about the Hindu tradition of arranged marriages.

	Words Read	Miscues

[Father] started talking as if we were all very small and he were | 13 | _____

conducting one of our "dinner-table-school" discussions. He | 20 | _____

said that by right and tradition the oldest daughter had to be | 32 | _____

given in marriage first, and that the ripe age for marriage was | 44 | _____

nineteen. He said that when a girl approached that age her | 55 | _____

parents, who had to take the initiative, made many inquiries and | 66 | _____

followed many leads. They investigated each young man and his | 76 | _____

family background, his relatives, his friends, his classmates, | 84 | _____

because it was important to know what kind of family the girl | 96 | _____

would be marrying into, what kind of company she would be | 107 | _____

expected to keep. If the girl's parents decided that a particular | 118 | _____

young man was suitable, then his people also had to make their | 130 | _____

investigations, but, however favorable their findings, their decision | 138 | _____

was unpredictable, because good, well-settled boys were in great | 147 | _____

demand and could afford to be choosy. All this took a lot of time. | 161 | _____

"That's why I said nothing to you children about why I went to | 174 | _____

Mussoorie," he concluded. "I went to see a young man for Pom. | 186 | _____

She's already nineteen." | 189 | _____

We were stunned. We have never really faced the idea that | 200 | _____

Sister Pom might get married and suddenly leave, I thought. | 210 | _____

Needs Work   1   2   3   4   5   Excellent
Paid attention to punctuation

Needs Work   1   2   3   4   5   Excellent
Sounded good

Total Words Read _____

Total Errors − _____

Correct WPM _____

Jumping the Bar:
Arabella Mansfield

Nonfiction

Read about how a woman fought for and won the right to
practice law in the United States.

First Reading

	Words Read	Miscues

Upon her admission to the Iowa bar in 1869, Arabella | 10 | _____
Mansfield became the first woman given official sanction to | 19 | _____
practice law in the United States. In fact, she was the first in | 32 | _____
Europe or North America. In Canada a woman was first admitted | 43 | _____
to the bar in 1897. France did not accept women lawyers until | 55 | _____
1900. England and Ireland qualified their first women lawyers in | 65 | _____
1922. Although Mansfield never argued a case in court or took | 76 | _____
on clients, she opened the door to women who would follow. | 87 | _____

Mansfield was born Belle Aurelia Babb in Iowa in 1846. | 97 | _____
She studied law on her own and then passed the Iowa bar | 109 | _____
examination, despite a statute that limited admission to "white | 118 | _____
male" residents of the state. The Iowa Supreme Court ruled that | 129 | _____
language that appears to stipulate men can be understood to | 139 | _____
include women. What looked like a legal restriction could not be | 150 | _____
used to deny women admittance to the bar and therefore to the | 162 | _____
practice of law. This decision was cited in later court cases filed | 174 | _____
on behalf of women attempting to join the bar in other states. | 186 | _____

Mansfield went on to a distinguished career as a college | 196 | _____
professor. She was also a founding member of the Iowa Woman | 207 | _____
Suffrage Society. She died in 1911 at the age of 65. | 218 | _____

Needs Work 1 2 3 4 5 Excellent
Paid attention to punctuation

Needs Work 1 2 3 4 5 Excellent
Sounded good

Total Words Read _____

Total Errors − _____

Correct WPM _____

Jumping the Bar:
Arabella Mansfield

Read about how a woman fought for and won the right to
practice law in the United States.

	Words Read	Miscues
Upon her admission to the Iowa bar in 1869, Arabella	10	_____
Mansfield became the first woman given official sanction to	19	_____
practice law in the United States. In fact, she was the first in	32	_____
Europe or North America. In Canada a woman was first admitted	43	_____
to the bar in 1897. France did not accept women lawyers until	55	_____
1900. England and Ireland qualified their first women lawyers in	65	_____
1922. Although Mansfield never argued a case in court or took	76	_____
on clients, she opened the door to women who would follow.	87	_____
Mansfield was born Belle Aurelia Babb in Iowa in 1846.	97	_____
She studied law on her own and then passed the Iowa bar	109	_____
examination, despite a statute that limited admission to "white	118	_____
male" residents of the state. The Iowa Supreme Court ruled that	129	_____
language that appears to stipulate men can be understood to	139	_____
include women. What looked like a legal restriction could not be	150	_____
used to deny women admittance to the bar and therefore to the	162	_____
practice of law. This decision was cited in later court cases filed	174	_____
on behalf of women attempting to join the bar in other states.	186	_____
Mansfield went on to a distinguished career as a college	196	_____
professor. She was also a founding member of the Iowa Woman	207	_____
Suffrage Society. She died in 1911 at the age of 65.	218	_____

Needs Work   1   2   3   4   5   Excellent
Paid attention to punctuation

Needs Work   1   2   3   4   5   Excellent
Sounded good

Total Words Read _____

Total Errors − _____

Correct WPM _____

42
Fiction

from "The Winner"
by Barbara Kimenye

Look in on the lottery winner as his close friends and relatives
help him celebrate his wonderful luck.

First Reading

	Words Read	Miscues

Nantondo hung about long enough to have her picture taken | 10 | _____

with Pius. Or rather, she managed to slip beside him just as the | 23 | _____

cameras clicked, and so it was that every Uganda newspaper, on | 34 | _____

the following day, carried a front-page photograph of "Mr. Pius | 44 | _____

Ndawula and his happy wife," a caption that caused Pius to shake | 56 | _____

with rage and threaten legal proceedings, but over which Nantondo | 66 | _____

gloated as she proudly showed it to everybody she visited. | 76 | _____

"Tell us, Mr. Ndawula, what do you intend to do with all the | 89 | _____

money you have won . . . ? | 93 | _____

"Tell us, Mr. Ndawula, how often have you completed | 102 | _____

[football] pools coupons . . . ? | 105 | _____

"Tell us . . . Tell us . . . Tell us . . ." | 111 | _____

Pius's head was reeling under this bombardment of questions, | 120 | _____

and he was even more confused by Salongo's constant nudging | 130 | _____

and muttered advice to "Say nothing!" Nor did the relatives make | 141 | _____

things easier. Their persistent clamoring for his attention, and the | 151 | _____

way they kept shoving their children under his nose, made it | 162 | _____

impossible for him to think, let alone talk. | 170 | _____

It isn't at all easy, when you have lived for sixty-five years in | 183 | _____

complete obscurity, to adjust yourself in a matter of hours to the | 195 | _____

role of a celebrity, and the strain was beginning to tell. | 206 | _____

Needs Work   1   2   3   4   5   Excellent
Paid attention to punctuation

Needs Work   1   2   3   4   5   Excellent
Sounded good

Total Words Read _____

Total Errors − _____

Correct WPM _____

42
Fiction

from **"The Winner"**
by Barbara Kimenye

Look in on the lottery winner as his close friends and relatives
help him celebrate his wonderful luck.

	Words Read	Miscues
Nantondo hung about long enough to have her picture taken	10	_____
with Pius. Or rather, she managed to slip beside him just as the	23	_____
cameras clicked, and so it was that every Uganda newspaper, on	34	_____
the following day, carried a front-page photograph of "Mr. Pius	44	_____
Ndawula and his happy wife," a caption that caused Pius to shake	56	_____
with rage and threaten legal proceedings, but over which Nantondo	66	_____
gloated as she proudly showed it to everybody she visited.	76	_____
"Tell us, Mr. Ndawula, what do you intend to do with all the	89	_____
money you have won . . . ?	93	_____
"Tell us, Mr. Ndawula, how often have you completed	102	_____
[football] pools coupons . . . ?	105	_____
"Tell us . . . Tell us . . . Tell us . . ."	111	_____
Pius's head was reeling under this bombardment of questions,	120	_____
and he was even more confused by Salongo's constant nudging	130	_____
and muttered advice to "Say nothing!" Nor did the relatives make	141	_____
things easier. Their persistent clamoring for his attention, and the	151	_____
way they kept shoving their children under his nose, made it	162	_____
impossible for him to think, let alone talk.	170	_____
It isn't at all easy, when you have lived for sixty-five years in	183	_____
complete obscurity, to adjust yourself in a matter of hours to the	195	_____
role of a celebrity, and the strain was beginning to tell.	206	_____

Needs Work   1 2 3 4 5   Excellent
Paid attention to punctuation

Needs Work   1 2 3 4 5   Excellent
Sounded good

Total Words Read _____

Total Errors − _____

Correct WPM _____

43

Fiction

from *Arabian Jazz*
by Diana Abu-Jaber

Connect with the drummer Matussem and the reason he keeps a
continuous beat.

First Reading

	Words Read	Miscues

[Matussem] had become increasingly bemused over the years, — 8 _____

wandering into abstraction, traveling in and out of conversations — 17 _____

like a visitor to foreign places. Only at his drums did he seem to — 31 _____

focus, concentrate with the purpose of remembering, steering — 39 _____

rhythms into line, coaxing a steady—in his word, *peripatetic*— — 49 _____

pulse out of air. — 53 _____

His wife's face was imprinted on his consciousness. He — 62 _____

thought of her as he drove to work in the mornings through ice — 75 _____

and rain. His sense of loss was sometimes so potent that he — 87 _____

became disoriented. His need to drum grew sharp as a knife cut; — 99 _____

he tapped and shuffled behind his desk. He made his secretaries — 110 _____

nervous, and visitors to his office would stay for only the briefest — 122 _____

sessions until the tapping became too much. Matussem's — 130 _____

daughters, Jemorah and Melvina, could tell when he was really — 140 _____

napping—not just feigning sleep to eavesdrop—because his feet — 150 _____

would start jerking rhythmically, tapping out time to Charlie — 159 _____

Parker. After their mother's death, they heard him both mornings — 169 _____

and evenings, alone or with his band, tapping in the basement, — 180 _____

drums humming, tripping and rushing, giddy, loud-voiced. This — 188 _____

sound had followed the girls through the years, from their father's — 199 _____

first riffs on a child's kit he'd found in the basement to the Snazzy — 213 _____

Sound of Mat Ramoud and the Ramoudettes. — 220 _____

Needs Work   1 2 3 4 5   Excellent
Paid attention to punctuation

Needs Work   1 2 3 4 5   Excellent
Sounded good

Total Words Read _____

Total Errors − _____

Correct WPM _____

43 from *Arabian Jazz*

Fiction by Diana Abu-Jaber

Connect with the drummer Matussem and the reason he keeps a continuous beat.

〜〜〜

[Matussem] had become increasingly bemused over the years,	8 _____
wandering into abstraction, traveling in and out of conversations	17 _____
like a visitor to foreign places. Only at his drums did he seem to	31 _____
focus, concentrate with the purpose of remembering, steering	39 _____
rhythms into line, coaxing a steady—in his word, *peripatetic*—	49 _____
pulse out of air.	53 _____

His wife's face was imprinted on his consciousness. He thought of her as he drove to work in the mornings through ice and rain. His sense of loss was sometimes so potent that he became disoriented. His need to drum grew sharp as a knife cut; he tapped and shuffled behind his desk. He made his secretaries nervous, and visitors to his office would stay for only the briefest sessions until the tapping became too much. Matussem's daughters, Jemorah and Melvina, could tell when he was really napping—not just feigning sleep to eavesdrop—because his feet would start jerking rhythmically, tapping out time to Charlie Parker. After their mother's death, they heard him both mornings and evenings, alone or with his band, tapping in the basement, drums humming, tripping and rushing, giddy, loud-voiced. This sound had followed the girls through the years, from their father's first riffs on a child's kit he'd found in the basement to the Snazzy Sound of Mat Ramoud and the Ramoudettes.

62, 75, 87, 99, 110, 122, 130, 140, 150, 159, 169, 180, 188, 199, 213, 220

Needs Work   1   2   3   4   5   Excellent
Paid attention to punctuation

Needs Work   1   2   3   4   5   Excellent
Sounded good

Total Words Read _____

Total Errors − _____

Correct WPM _____

44

Nonfiction

from "The United States vs. Susan B. Anthony"

by Margaret Truman

Learn about one incident in the early struggle for women's right to vote.

∞∞∞

	Words Read	Miscues
Susan B. Anthony felt perfectly justified in concluding that the	10	_____
right to vote was among the privileges of citizenship and that it	22	_____
extended to women as well as men. I'm sure she must have also	35	_____
seen the humor of outwitting the supposedly superior males who	45	_____
wrote the Amendment.	48	_____
It was bad enough for a bunch of women to barge into one	61	_____
sacred male precinct—the barber shop—but to insist on being	72	_____
admitted to another holy of holies—the voting booth—was	82	_____
absolutely outrageous. Moustaches twitched, throats were cleared,	89	_____
a whispered conference was held in the corner.	97	_____
Susan had brought along a copy of the Fourteenth	106	_____
Amendment. She read it aloud, carefully pointing out to the men	117	_____
in charge of registration that the document failed to state that the	129	_____
privilege of voting extended only to males.	136	_____
Only one man in the barber shop had the nerve to refuse the	149	_____
Anthony sisters the right to register. The rest buckled under	159	_____
Susan's determined oratory and allowed them to sign the huge,	169	_____
leather-bound voter registration book. If the men in the barber	179	_____
shop thought they were getting rid of a little band of crackpots	191	_____
the easy way, they were wrong. Susan urged all her followers in	203	_____
Rochester to register.	206	_____

Needs Work   1 2 3 4 5   Excellent
Paid attention to punctuation

Needs Work   1 2 3 4 5   Excellent
Sounded good

Total Words Read _____

Total Errors − _____

Correct WPM _____

from "**The United States vs. Susan B. Anthony**"

by Margaret Truman

Learn about one incident in the early struggle for women's right to vote.

Second Reading

	Words Read	Miscues

Susan B. Anthony felt perfectly justified in concluding that the 10 _____

right to vote was among the privileges of citizenship and that it 22 _____

extended to women as well as men. I'm sure she must have also 35 _____

seen the humor of outwitting the supposedly superior males who 45 _____

wrote the Amendment. 48 _____

It was bad enough for a bunch of women to barge into one 61 _____

sacred male precinct—the barber shop—but to insist on being 72 _____

admitted to another holy of holies—the voting booth—was 82 _____

absolutely outrageous. Moustaches twitched, throats were cleared, 89 _____

a whispered conference was held in the corner. 97 _____

Susan had brought along a copy of the Fourteenth 106 _____

Amendment. She read it aloud, carefully pointing out to the men 117 _____

in charge of registration that the document failed to state that the 129 _____

privilege of voting extended only to males. 136 _____

Only one man in the barber shop had the nerve to refuse the 149 _____

Anthony sisters the right to register. The rest buckled under 159 _____

Susan's determined oratory and allowed them to sign the huge, 169 _____

leather-bound voter registration book. If the men in the barber 179 _____

shop thought they were getting rid of a little band of crackpots 191 _____

the easy way, they were wrong. Susan urged all her followers in 203 _____

Rochester to register. 206 _____

Needs Work 1 2 3 4 5 Excellent
Paid attention to punctuation

Needs Work 1 2 3 4 5 Excellent
Sounded good

Total Words Read _____

Total Errors − _____

Correct WPM _____

45 A Brief History of the Bicycle

Nonfiction

Learn about the development of the bicycle.

First Reading

	Words Read	Miscues

	Words Read	Miscues
At the end of the eighteenth century, a French gentleman was	11	_____
observed on a two-wheeled conveyance, propelling himself by	19	_____
pushing his feet against the ground. Before long, people were	29	_____
devising ways to make this primitive bicycle an effective means	39	_____
of transportation.	41	_____
Although a number of models preceded it, the "boneshaker,"	50	_____
built in 1863, is generally considered to be the first successful	61	_____
bicycle. A stiff frame and metal-rimmed wheels produced the	70	_____
unpleasant, jarring ride from which it takes its nickname. Its	80	_____
official name was the velocipede.	85	_____
The next innovation was the highwheeler, a bicycle with an	95	_____
immense front wheel and a small rear wheel. It offered a more	107	_____
comfortable ride than the velocipede, but it was difficult to mount	118	_____
and dangerous to operate. In fact, the phrase "take a header"	129	_____
originated as a description of falling head first from the	139	_____
highwheeler's seat.	141	_____
By the 1880s, however, manufacturers had returned to a	150	_____
design that featured wheels of equal size. They also made bicycles	161	_____
more powerful by connecting the pedals to the rear wheels with a	173	_____
chain. Pushing on the pedals not only made the front wheel go	185	_____
around but rotated the rear wheel as well.	193	_____
Since that time, better materials that make a stronger frame,	203	_____
springs and pneumatic tires that cushion shocks from the road,	213	_____
and improved safety features have enhanced this basic design.	222	_____

Needs Work   1   2   3   4   5   Excellent
      Paid attention to punctuation

Needs Work   1   2   3   4   5   Excellent
      Sounded good

Total Words Read _____

Total Errors − _____

Correct WPM _____

A Brief History of the Bicycle

Learn about the development of the bicycle.

	Words Read	Miscues
At the end of the eighteenth century, a French gentleman was	11	_____
observed on a two-wheeled conveyance, propelling himself by	19	_____
pushing his feet against the ground. Before long, people were	29	_____
devising ways to make this primitive bicycle an effective means	39	_____
of transportation.	41	_____
Although a number of models preceded it, the "boneshaker,"	50	_____
built in 1863, is generally considered to be the first successful	61	_____
bicycle. A stiff frame and metal-rimmed wheels produced the	70	_____
unpleasant, jarring ride from which it takes its nickname. Its	80	_____
official name was the velocipede.	85	_____
The next innovation was the highwheeler, a bicycle with an	95	_____
immense front wheel and a small rear wheel. It offered a more	107	_____
comfortable ride than the velocipede, but it was difficult to mount	118	_____
and dangerous to operate. In fact, the phrase "take a header"	129	_____
originated as a description of falling head first from the	139	_____
highwheeler's seat.	141	_____
By the 1880s, however, manufacturers had returned to a	150	_____
design that featured wheels of equal size. They also made bicycles	161	_____
more powerful by connecting the pedals to the rear wheels with a	173	_____
chain. Pushing on the pedals not only made the front wheel go	185	_____
around but rotated the rear wheel as well.	193	_____
Since that time, better materials that make a stronger frame,	203	_____
springs and pneumatic tires that cushion shocks from the road,	213	_____
and improved safety features have enhanced this basic design.	222	_____

Needs Work   1   2   3   4   5   Excellent
———————————————————————
Paid attention to punctuation

Needs Work   1   2   3   4   5   Excellent
———————————————————————
Sounded good

Total Words Read   _____

Total Errors   −_____

Correct WPM   _____

46 from **"Seventeen Syllables"**

Fiction by Hisaye Yamamoto

First Reading

Learn about *haiku* in this passage about a young woman who tries to please her mother.

	Words Read	Miscues

	Words Read	Miscues
The first Rosie knew that her mother had taken to writing	11	_____
poems was one evening when she finished one and read it aloud	23	_____
for her daughter's approval. It was about cats, and Rosie	33	_____
pretended to understand it thoroughly and appreciate it no end,	43	_____
partly because she hesitated to disillusion her mother about the	53	_____
quantity and quality of Japanese she had learned in all the years	65	_____
now that she had been going to Japanese school every Saturday	76	_____
(and Wednesday, too, in the summer). Even so, her mother must	87	_____
have been skeptical about the depth of Rosie's understanding,	96	_____
because she explained afterwards about the kind of poem she was	107	_____
trying to write.	110	_____
See, Rosie, she said, it was a *haiku*, a poem in which she must	124	_____
pack all her meaning into seventeen syllables only, which were	134	_____
divided into three lines of five, seven, and five syllables. In the	146	_____
one she had just read, she had tried to capture the charm of a	160	_____
kitten, as well as comment on the superstition that owning a cat	172	_____
of three colors meant good luck.	178	_____
"Yes, yes, I understand. How utterly lovely," Rosie said, and her	189	_____
mother, either satisfied or seeing through the deception and	198	_____
resigned, went back to composing.	203	_____

Needs Work 1 2 3 4 5 Excellent
Paid attention to punctuation

Needs Work 1 2 3 4 5 Excellent
Sounded good

Total Words Read _____

Total Errors − _____

Correct WPM _____

from "Seventeen Syllables"

by Hisaye Yamamoto

Learn about *haiku* in this passage about a young woman who tries to please her mother.

	Words Read	Miscues

The first Rosie knew that her mother had taken to writing | 11 | _____

poems was one evening when she finished one and read it aloud | 23 | _____

for her daughter's approval. It was about cats, and Rosie | 33 | _____

pretended to understand it thoroughly and appreciate it no end, | 43 | _____

partly because she hesitated to disillusion her mother about the | 53 | _____

quantity and quality of Japanese she had learned in all the years | 65 | _____

now that she had been going to Japanese school every Saturday | 76 | _____

(and Wednesday, too, in the summer). Even so, her mother must | 87 | _____

have been skeptical about the depth of Rosie's understanding, | 96 | _____

because she explained afterwards about the kind of poem she was | 107 | _____

trying to write. | 110 | _____

See, Rosie, she said, it was a *haiku*, a poem in which she must | 124 | _____

pack all her meaning into seventeen syllables only, which were | 134 | _____

divided into three lines of five, seven, and five syllables. In the | 146 | _____

one she had just read, she had tried to capture the charm of a | 160 | _____

kitten, as well as comment on the superstition that owning a cat | 172 | _____

of three colors meant good luck. | 178 | _____

"Yes, yes, I understand. How utterly lovely," Rosie said, and her | 189 | _____

mother, either satisfied or seeing through the deception and | 198 | _____

resigned, went back to composing. | 203 | _____

Needs Work   1   2   3   4   5   Excellent
Paid attention to punctuation

Needs Work   1   2   3   4   5   Excellent
Sounded good

Total Words Read   _____

Total Errors   − _____

Correct WPM   _____

47

Fiction

from "Silent Snow, Secret Snow"

by Conrad Aiken

Recognize that sometimes keeping a secret can be even more precious than the secret itself.

First Reading

	Words Read	Miscues

Just why it should have happened, or why it should have / 11 / _____
happened just when it did, he could not, of course, possibly have / 23 / _____
said; nor perhaps could it even have occurred to him to ask. The / 36 / _____
thing was above all a secret, something to be preciously concealed / 47 / _____
from Mother and Father; and to that very fact it owed an / 59 / _____
enormous part of its deliciousness. It was like a peculiarly / 69 / _____
beautiful trinket to be carried unmentioned in one's trouser / 78 / _____
pocket—a rare stamp, an old coin, a few tiny gold links found / 91 / _____
trodden out of shape on the path in the park, a pebble of / 104 / _____
carnelian, a sea shell distinguishable from all others by an unusual / 115 / _____
spot or stripe—and, as if it were any one of these, he carried / 129 / _____
around with him everywhere a warm and persistent and / 138 / _____
increasingly beautiful sense of possession. Nor was it only a sense / 149 / _____
of possession—it was also a sense of protection. It was as if, in / 163 / _____
some delightful way, his secret gave him a fortress, a wall behind / 175 / _____
which he could retreat into heavenly seclusion. This was almost / 185 / _____
the first thing he had noticed about it—apart from the oddness of / 198 / _____
the thing itself. / 201 / _____

Needs Work   1   2   3   4   5   Excellent
_____
Paid attention to punctuation

Needs Work   1   2   3   4   5   Excellent
_____
Sounded good

Total Words Read _____

Total Errors − _____

Correct WPM _____

47

Fiction

from **"Silent Snow, Secret Snow"**

by Conrad Aiken

Recognize that sometimes keeping a secret can be even more precious than the secret itself.

Just why it should have happened, or why it should have	11	_____
happened just when it did, he could not, of course, possibly have	23	_____
said; nor perhaps could it even have occurred to him to ask. The	36	_____
thing was above all a secret, something to be preciously concealed	47	_____
from Mother and Father; and to that very fact it owed an	59	_____
enormous part of its deliciousness. It was like a peculiarly	69	_____
beautiful trinket to be carried unmentioned in one's trouser	78	_____
pocket—a rare stamp, an old coin, a few tiny gold links found	91	_____
trodden out of shape on the path in the park, a pebble of	104	_____
carnelian, a sea shell distinguishable from all others by an unusual	115	_____
spot or stripe—and, as if it were any one of these, he carried	129	_____
around with him everywhere a warm and persistent and	138	_____
increasingly beautiful sense of possession. Nor was it only a sense	149	_____
of possession—it was also a sense of protection. It was as if, in	163	_____
some delightful way, his secret gave him a fortress, a wall behind	175	_____
which he could retreat into heavenly seclusion. This was almost	185	_____
the first thing he had noticed about it—apart from the oddness of	198	_____
the thing itself.	201	_____

Needs Work   1   2   3   4   5   Excellent
_____
Paid attention to punctuation

Needs Work   1   2   3   4   5   Excellent
_____
Sounded good

Total Words Read _____

Total Errors − _____

Correct WPM _____

48 Georgia O'Keeffe

Read about how a New York painter found a new perspective in the West.

First Reading

	Words Read	Miscues

The artist Georgia O'Keeffe was born in Wisconsin, was — 9 _____

brought up in Virginia, and lived much of her adult life in New — 22 _____

York City. The place she loved most, however, was New Mexico. — 33 _____

O'Keeffe had first visited New Mexico in 1917 while on — 43 _____

vacation with her sister. In 1929 she returned at the invitation of — 55 _____

writer Mabel Dodge Luhan. The landscape, the light, and most — 65 _____

of all the solitude suited O'Keeffe's rather quiet temperament — 74 _____

perfectly. The paintings for which she was already famous were — 84 _____

simple, almost abstract, portrayals of skyscrapers and flowers, — 92 _____

vibrant canvases filled with color harmonies. In New Mexico, she — 102 _____

discovered new themes to inspire her: the reddish contours of the — 113 _____

mountains, the flame-tinted spikes of jimson weed, the curve of — 123 _____

an adobe dwelling, and the bleached animal bones retrieved from — 133 _____

the desert. — 135 _____

Every summer for almost two decades, O'Keeffe traveled to — 144 _____

New Mexico, either renting a house or staying with friends. In — 155 _____

1940 she purchased the old Ghost Ranch. About five years later, — 166 _____

she acquired an abandoned adobe compound and some land. — 175 _____

In 1949, three years after the death of her husband, she — 186 _____

moved to New Mexico permanently. — 191 _____

O'Keeffe painted for many years, stopping only when she — 200 _____

became almost blind. She died in 1986 at the age of 99. — 212 _____

Needs Work   1 2 3 4 5   Excellent
Paid attention to punctuation

Needs Work   1 2 3 4 5   Excellent
Sounded good

Total Words Read _____

Total Errors − _____

Correct WPM _____

48 Georgia O'Keeffe

Nonfiction

Read about how a New York painter found a new perspective
in the West.

The artist Georgia O'Keeffe was born in Wisconsin, was	9
brought up in Virginia, and lived much of her adult life in New	22
York City. The place she loved most, however, was New Mexico.	33
O'Keeffe had first visited New Mexico in 1917 while on	43
vacation with her sister. In 1929 she returned at the invitation of	55
writer Mabel Dodge Luhan. The landscape, the light, and most	65
of all the solitude suited O'Keeffe's rather quiet temperament	74
perfectly. The paintings for which she was already famous were	84
simple, almost abstract, portrayals of skyscrapers and flowers,	92
vibrant canvases filled with color harmonies. In New Mexico, she	102
discovered new themes to inspire her: the reddish contours of the	113
mountains, the flame-tinted spikes of jimson weed, the curve of	123
an adobe dwelling, and the bleached animal bones retrieved from	133
the desert.	135
Every summer for almost two decades, O'Keeffe traveled to	144
New Mexico, either renting a house or staying with friends. In	155
1940 she purchased the old Ghost Ranch. About five years later,	166
she acquired an abandoned adobe compound and some land.	175
In 1949, three years after the death of her husband, she	186
moved to New Mexico permanently.	191
O'Keeffe painted for many years, stopping only when she	200
became almost blind. She died in 1986 at the age of 99.	212

Needs Work   1   2   3   4   5   Excellent
  Paid attention to punctuation

Needs Work   1   2   3   4   5   Excellent
  Sounded good

Total Words Read _____

Total Errors – _____

Correct WPM _____

49 Norman Rockwell and the Four Freedoms

Nonfiction

Discover what inspired the artist to create one of his most famous series of paintings.

∞∞∞

	Words Read	Miscues

First Reading

	Words Read	Miscues
Norman Rockwell's art has been dismissed by some as mere	10	_____
illustration and lionized by others as the purest expression of the	21	_____
American character. Born in New York City in 1894, Rockwell	31	_____
studied at several New York art schools. His skills as a draftsman	43	_____
and his thorough familiarity with the art of the great masters	54	_____
helped him achieve early success as a magazine illustrator.	63	_____
On January 6, 1941, President Franklin D. Roosevelt	71	_____
described four basic human freedoms in his State of the Union	82	_____
address to Congress: freedom of speech and expression, freedom	91	_____
of worship, freedom from want, and freedom from fear. Inspired	101	_____
by these words, Rockwell created four paintings in 1943 that he	112	_____
called The Four Freedoms series.	117	_____
The paintings express complex ideas through simple images.	125	_____
Freedom of Speech, for instance, illustrates a New England town	135	_____
meeting in which a citizen is presenting his opinion. *Freedom from*	146	_____
Want shows a family gathered around the holiday table as the	157	_____
mother sets down an immense roasted turkey.	164	_____
The *Saturday Evening Post* magazine first reproduced the	172	_____
paintings. The originals were later exhibited throughout the United	181	_____
States, raising more than $130 million through the sale of war	192	_____
bonds, to support the country in World War II.	201	_____

Needs Work   1   2   3   4   5   Excellent
           Paid attention to punctuation

Needs Work   1   2   3   4   5   Excellent
           Sounded good

Total Words Read _____

Total Errors − _____

Correct WPM _____

Norman Rockwell and the Four Freedoms

Discover what inspired the artist to create one of his most famous series of paintings.

	Words Read	Miscues

Norman Rockwell's art has been dismissed by some as mere | 10 | _____

illustration and lionized by others as the purest expression of the | 21 | _____

American character. Born in New York City in 1894, Rockwell | 31 | _____

studied at several New York art schools. His skills as a draftsman | 43 | _____

and his thorough familiarity with the art of the great masters | 54 | _____

helped him achieve early success as a magazine illustrator. | 63 | _____

On January 6, 1941, President Franklin D. Roosevelt | 71 | _____

described four basic human freedoms in his State of the Union | 82 | _____

address to Congress: freedom of speech and expression, freedom | 91 | _____

of worship, freedom from want, and freedom from fear. Inspired | 101 | _____

by these words, Rockwell created four paintings in 1943 that he | 112 | _____

called The Four Freedoms series. | 117 | _____

The paintings express complex ideas through simple images. | 125 | _____

Freedom of Speech, for instance, illustrates a New England town | 135 | _____

meeting in which a citizen is presenting his opinion. *Freedom from* | 146 | _____

Want shows a family gathered around the holiday table as the | 157 | _____

mother sets down an immense roasted turkey. | 164 | _____

The *Saturday Evening Post* magazine first reproduced the | 172 | _____

paintings. The originals were later exhibited throughout the United | 181 | _____

States, raising more than $130 million through the sale of war | 192 | _____

bonds, to support the country in World War II. | 201 | _____

Needs Work   1   2   3   4   5   Excellent
Paid attention to punctuation

Needs Work   1   2   3   4   5   Excellent
Sounded good

Total Words Read _____

Total Errors − _____

Correct WPM _____

50

Nonfiction

from *The New Country*
by Richard A. Bartlett

Read about the American pioneers who settled the Ohio River
Valley in the early 19th century.

First Reading

	Words Read	Miscues
The Americans looked down upon the wide Ohio and the still	11	_____
wider Mississippi, the waters still fresh and, even if muddy, hardly	22	_____
noxious or polluted, and saw only nature and beauty. On either	33	_____
side stretched the great forest, with butternut, tulip tree, black	43	_____
willow, cherry, mulberry, and plum growing along the banks.	52	_____
Occasionally the woods thinned out; in these "wood pastures," as	62	_____
the pioneers called them, deer could be seen peacefully grazing.	72	_____
Farther up on the hillsides grew red, white, and black oak, hickory,	84	_____
walnut, ash, poplar, and sycamore.	89	_____
Those who came to the new country by flatboat would	99	_____
sometimes pole and pull their loaded arks up a small tributary	110	_____
stream until they found their homestead site, but were more likely	121	_____
to pull into a riverside community, such as Cincinnati or Marietta,	132	_____
or Limestone or Louisville, sell their boat for lumber, and then	143	_____
make their way inland. Their flatboat had contained the	152	_____
paraphernalia of a farm, after all, with dismantled wagon, horse,	162	_____
family cow, pigs, chickens, and dogs. When the ark was sold, the	174	_____
wheels were attached to the wagon, the box loaded with the	185	_____
pioneer's [goods], and again the party was on its way inland.	196	_____

Needs Work   1 2 3 4 5   Excellent
        Paid attention to punctuation

Needs Work   1 2 3 4 5   Excellent
        Sounded good

Total Words Read _____

Total Errors − _____

Correct WPM _____

50

from *The New Country*

by Richard A. Bartlett

Read about the American pioneers who settled the Ohio River Valley in the early 19th century.

Second Reading

	Words Read	Miscues
The Americans looked down upon the wide Ohio and the still	11	_____
wider Mississippi, the waters still fresh and, even if muddy, hardly	22	_____
noxious or polluted, and saw only nature and beauty. On either	33	_____
side stretched the great forest, with butternut, tulip tree, black	43	_____
willow, cherry, mulberry, and plum growing along the banks.	52	_____
Occasionally the woods thinned out; in these "wood pastures," as	62	_____
the pioneers called them, deer could be seen peacefully grazing.	72	_____
Farther up on the hillsides grew red, white, and black oak, hickory,	84	_____
walnut, ash, poplar, and sycamore.	89	_____
Those who came to the new country by flatboat would	99	_____
sometimes pole and pull their loaded arks up a small tributary	110	_____
stream until they found their homestead site, but were more likely	121	_____
to pull into a riverside community, such as Cincinnati or Marietta,	132	_____
or Limestone or Louisville, sell their boat for lumber, and then	143	_____
make their way inland. Their flatboat had contained the	152	_____
paraphernalia of a farm, after all, with dismantled wagon, horse,	162	_____
family cow, pigs, chickens, and dogs. When the ark was sold, the	174	_____
wheels were attached to the wagon, the box loaded with the	185	_____
pioneer's [goods], and again the party was on its way inland.	196	_____

Needs Work   1   2   3   4   5   Excellent
Paid attention to punctuation

Needs Work   1   2   3   4   5   Excellent
Sounded good

Total Words Read _____

Total Errors − _____

Correct WPM _____

51

Fiction

from "Good Will"

by Jane Smiley

Discover Robert Miller just before he is interviewed about how he built his self-sufficient family farm.

	Words Read	Miscues
My promise to [my wife] was that Tina wouldn't ask her any	12	_____
questions and that she and Tommy wouldn't have to appear in	23	_____
any photographs.	25	_____
The fact is, I should like this unaccustomed view of the	36	_____
Miller family, Robert, Elizabeth, and Thomas, on their small	45	_____
but remarkably productive acreage just outside Moreton,	52	_____
Pennsylvania. The fact is that years ago, when I had first bought	64	_____
the land and was building the big compost heaps behind the	75	_____
chicken shed, I used to imagine some interviewer just like Tina	86	_____
passing through, showing just her degree of dignity, respectability,	95	_____
and knowledgeable interest. I used to plan how I would guide her	107	_____
around the beds, then undug, show her through the house, then	118	_____
unbuilt, seat her in the chairs, feed her off the table, entertain her	131	_____
on the porch, and through imagining her, I saw all the details	143	_____
she might like. I imagined I would tell her, as I did during the	157	_____
interview, that imagination itself was the key—once I knew what	168	_____
it was specifically that I wanted, then either I would build it or it	182	_____
would turn up. And here she is, though I stopped looking for her	195	_____
long ago, right on schedule, reacting as she was destined to react.	207	_____

Needs Work   1   2   3   4   5   Excellent
_____
Paid attention to punctuation

Needs Work   1   2   3   4   5   Excellent
_____
Sounded good

Total Words Read _____

Total Errors − _____

Correct WPM _____

51

Fiction

from "Good Will"

by Jane Smiley

Discover Robert Miller just before he is interviewed about how he built his self-sufficient family farm.

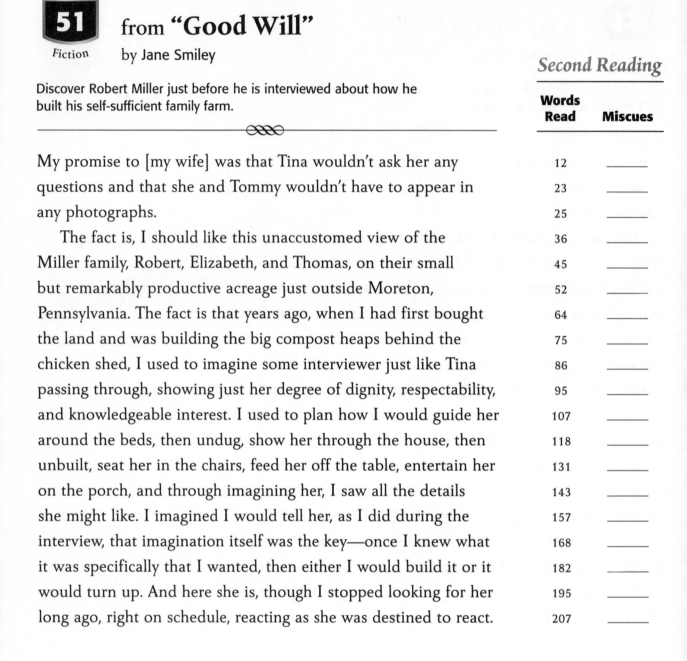

	Words Read	Miscues
My promise to [my wife] was that Tina wouldn't ask her any	12	_____
questions and that she and Tommy wouldn't have to appear in	23	_____
any photographs.	25	_____
The fact is, I should like this unaccustomed view of the	36	_____
Miller family, Robert, Elizabeth, and Thomas, on their small	45	_____
but remarkably productive acreage just outside Moreton,	52	_____
Pennsylvania. The fact is that years ago, when I had first bought	64	_____
the land and was building the big compost heaps behind the	75	_____
chicken shed, I used to imagine some interviewer just like Tina	86	_____
passing through, showing just her degree of dignity, respectability,	95	_____
and knowledgeable interest. I used to plan how I would guide her	107	_____
around the beds, then undug, show her through the house, then	118	_____
unbuilt, seat her in the chairs, feed her off the table, entertain her	131	_____
on the porch, and through imagining her, I saw all the details	143	_____
she might like. I imagined I would tell her, as I did during the	157	_____
interview, that imagination itself was the key—once I knew what	168	_____
it was specifically that I wanted, then either I would build it or it	182	_____
would turn up. And here she is, though I stopped looking for her	195	_____
long ago, right on schedule, reacting as she was destined to react.	207	_____

Needs Work   1 2 3 4 5   Excellent
Paid attention to punctuation

Needs Work   1 2 3 4 5   Excellent
Sounded good

Total Words Read   _____

Total Errors − _____

Correct WPM   _____

52

Nonfiction

from *Silent Dancing:*
A Partial Remembrance of a Puerto Rican Childhood
by Judith Ortiz Cofer

Listen as the author describes how stories played an important role in her childhood.

First Reading

	Words Read	Miscues
Mamá still had three of her own children at home, ranging in	12	_____
age from a teenage daughter to my favorite uncle who was six	24	_____
months older than me.	28	_____
Our solitary life in New Jersey, where we spent our days inside	40	_____
a small dark apartment watching television and waiting for our	50	_____
father to come home on leave from the navy, had not prepared us	63	_____
for life in Mamá's house or for the multitude of cousins, aunts	75	_____
and uncles pulling us into their loud conversations and rough	85	_____
games. For the first few days my little brother kept his head firmly	98	_____
buried in my mother's neck, while I stayed relatively close to her;	110	_____
but being nearly six, and able to speak as loudly as anyone, I soon	124	_____
joined Mamá's tribe.	127	_____
In the last few weeks before the beginning of school, when it	139	_____
was too hot for cooking until it was almost dark and when	151	_____
mothers would not even let their boys go to the playgrounds and	163	_____
parks for fear of sunstroke, Mamá would lead us to the mango	175	_____
tree, there to spin the web of her *cuentos* over us, making us	188	_____
forget the heat, the mosquitos, our past in a foreign country, and	200	_____
even the threat of the first day of school looming just ahead.	212	_____

Needs Work   1 2 3 4 5   Excellent
Paid attention to punctuation

Needs Work   1 2 3 4 5   Excellent
Sounded good

Total Words Read _____

Total Errors − _____

Correct WPM _____

52

Nonfiction

from *Silent Dancing:*
A Partial Remembrance of a Puerto Rican Childhood

by Judith Ortiz Cofer

Listen as the author describes how stories played an important role in her childhood.

	Words Read	Miscues
Mamá still had three of her own children at home, ranging in	12	_____
age from a teenage daughter to my favorite uncle who was six	24	_____
months older than me.	28	_____
Our solitary life in New Jersey, where we spent our days inside	40	_____
a small dark apartment watching television and waiting for our	50	_____
father to come home on leave from the navy, had not prepared us	63	_____
for life in Mamá's house or for the multitude of cousins, aunts	75	_____
and uncles pulling us into their loud conversations and rough	85	_____
games. For the first few days my little brother kept his head firmly	98	_____
buried in my mother's neck, while I stayed relatively close to her;	110	_____
but being nearly six, and able to speak as loudly as anyone, I soon	124	_____
joined Mamá's tribe.	127	_____
In the last few weeks before the beginning of school, when it	139	_____
was too hot for cooking until it was almost dark and when	151	_____
mothers would not even let their boys go to the playgrounds and	163	_____
parks for fear of sunstroke, Mamá would lead us to the mango	175	_____
tree, there to spin the web of her *cuentos* over us, making us	188	_____
forget the heat, the mosquitos, our past in a foreign country, and	200	_____
even the threat of the first day of school looming just ahead.	212	_____

Needs Work   1 2 3 4 5   Excellent
Paid attention to punctuation

Needs Work   1 2 3 4 5   Excellent
Sounded good

Total Words Read _____

Total Errors − _____

Correct WPM _____

from *Brothers and Keepers*

by John Edgar Wideman

First Reading

Examine why taking a shorter route had made the author unready
to visit his brother.

	Words Read	Miscues

I'd arrived at Western Penitentiary in record time. Yet something — 10 — _____

was wrong. The new route transported me to the gates but — 21 — _____

I wasn't ready to pass through. Different streets, different — 30 — _____

buildings along the way hadn't done the trick, didn't have the — 41 — _____

power to take me where I needed to go because the journey to — 54 — _____

visit my brother in prison was not simply a matter of miles and — 67 — _____

minutes. Between Homewood and Woods Run, the flat, — 75 — _____

industrialized wasteland beside the river where the prison's — 83 — _____

hidden, there is a vast, uncharted space, a no-man's land where — 94 — _____

the traveler must begin to forget home and begin to remember — 105 — _____

the alien world inside "The Walls." At some point an invisible line — 117 — _____

is crossed, the rules change. Visitors must take leave of the — 128 — _____

certainties underpinning their everyday lives. — 133 — _____

    Using the parkway to reach Woods Run had become part of — 144 — _____

the ritual I depended upon to get me ready to see my brother. — 157 — _____

Huge green exit signs suspended over the highway, tires screaming — 167 — _____

on gouged patches of road surface, the darkness and — 176 — _____

claustrophobia of Squirrel Hill Tunnel, miles of abandoned — 184 — _____

steel-mill sheds, a mosque's golden cupola, paddle-wheeled — 191 — _____

pleasure boats moored at the riverbank, the scenes and — 200 — _____

sensations I catalogue now as I write were stepping stones. — 210 — _____

Needs Work 1 2 3 4 5 Excellent
        Paid attention to punctuation

Needs Work 1 2 3 4 5 Excellent
        Sounded good

Total Words Read _____

Total Errors − _____

Correct WPM _____

53 from *Brothers and Keepers*

by John Edgar Wideman

Examine why taking a shorter route had made the author unready
to visit his brother.

Second Reading

	Words Read	Miscues
I'd arrived at Western Penitentiary in record time. Yet something	10	_____
was wrong. The new route transported me to the gates but	21	_____
I wasn't ready to pass through. Different streets, different	30	_____
buildings along the way hadn't done the trick, didn't have the	41	_____
power to take me where I needed to go because the journey to	54	_____
visit my brother in prison was not simply a matter of miles and	67	_____
minutes. Between Homewood and Woods Run, the flat,	75	_____
industrialized wasteland beside the river where the prison's	83	_____
hidden, there is a vast, uncharted space, a no-man's land where	94	_____
the traveler must begin to forget home and begin to remember	105	_____
the alien world inside "The Walls." At some point an invisible line	117	_____
is crossed, the rules change. Visitors must take leave of the	128	_____
certainties underpinning their everyday lives.	133	_____
Using the parkway to reach Woods Run had become part of	144	_____
the ritual I depended upon to get me ready to see my brother.	157	_____
Huge green exit signs suspended over the highway, tires screaming	167	_____
on gouged patches of road surface, the darkness and	176	_____
claustrophobia of Squirrel Hill Tunnel, miles of abandoned	184	_____
steel-mill sheds, a mosque's golden cupola, paddle-wheeled	191	_____
pleasure boats moored at the riverbank, the scenes and	200	_____
sensations I catalogue now as I write were stepping stones.	210	_____

Needs Work 1 2 3 4 5 Excellent
Paid attention to punctuation

Needs Work 1 2 3 4 5 Excellent
Sounded good

Total Words Read _____

Total Errors − _____

Correct WPM _____

54

Nonfiction

from *Nothing to Do but Stay:*
My Pioneer Mother

by Carrie Young

Listen as the author recalls the close, loving influence of
her mother.

First Reading

	Words Read	Miscues

It always gave my mother pause when she visited Barney on — 11 —

the farm after her marriage and observed her hoeing the garden, — 22 —

hauling grain to market, culling chickens, candling eggs, and — 31 —

sticking hypodermic needles into pigs and sheep. My mother — 40 —

would arrive home bemused. *Seven years of college*, she would say, — 51 —

and if you wanted to count all of those summer sessions Barney — 63 —

had to attend to retain her teaching status, it would be more like — 76 —

nine. My mother would hasten to add that she had nothing — 87 —

against farmers, farmers were the best; it was just that Barney had — 99 —

struggled longer and harder for her education than any of her — 110 —

other children, and now she could have reaped the rewards of the — 122 —

independence she had earned to make her life *easier*, instead of — 133 —

taking on the kind of hard work that she herself had always had — 146 —

. . . and then my mother's voice would trail off. — 154 —

My mother died before she knew how her thirteen — 163 —

grandchildren turned out, before she could know how they took — 173 —

to higher education like ducks to water. She would love to have — 185 —

toted up all of their advanced degrees, and if she could have — 197 —

watched their progress as they espoused one recondite profession — 206 —

after another, she would have been very proud. — 214 —

Needs Work   1   2   3   4   5   Excellent
Paid attention to punctuation

Needs Work   1   2   3   4   5   Excellent
Sounded good

Total Words Read _____

Total Errors − _____

Correct WPM _____

from *Nothing to Do but Stay:*
My Pioneer Mother
by Carrie Young

Listen as the author recalls the close, loving influence of her mother.

It always gave my mother pause when she visited Barney on — 11 _____

the farm after her marriage and observed her hoeing the garden, — 22 _____

hauling grain to market, culling chickens, candling eggs, and — 31 _____

sticking hypodermic needles into pigs and sheep. My mother — 40 _____

would arrive home bemused. *Seven years of college*, she would say, — 51 _____

and if you wanted to count all of those summer sessions Barney — 63 _____

had to attend to retain her teaching status, it would be more like — 76 _____

nine. My mother would hasten to add that she had nothing — 87 _____

against farmers, farmers were the best; it was just that Barney had — 99 _____

struggled longer and harder for her education than any of her — 110 _____

other children, and now she could have reaped the rewards of the — 122 _____

independence she had earned to make her life *easier*, instead of — 133 _____

taking on the kind of hard work that she herself had always had — 146 _____

. . . and then my mother's voice would trail off. — 154 _____

My mother died before she knew how her thirteen — 163 _____

grandchildren turned out, before she could know how they took — 173 _____

to higher education like ducks to water. She would love to have — 185 _____

toted up all of their advanced degrees, and if she could have — 197 _____

watched their progress as they espoused one recondite profession — 206 _____

after another, she would have been very proud. — 214 _____

Needs Work   1   2   3   4   5   Excellent
Paid attention to punctuation

Needs Work   1   2   3   4   5   Excellent
Sounded good

Total Words Read _____

Total Errors − _____

Correct WPM _____

55 from *In This Sign*

Fiction   by Joanne Greenberg

Discover that finding the perfect meaning of words can widen
your understanding of the world.

First Reading

	Words Read	Miscues

The newspaper had been an affectation at first, and a defense | 11 | _____
against having to stare at people on the bus, but since [Abel] had | 24 | _____
come to be a leader in the Deaf community and someone to be | 37 | _____
consulted, he had come to know the few well-educated Deaf, in | 48 | _____
the city, people who spelled more than they Signed because their | 59 | _____
needs and knowledges exceeded the Signs that were used for the | 70 | _____
basic things of living. More and more he felt himself needing to | 82 | _____
grow into these new words. How complicated they were! How | 92 | _____
minutely subtle the differences they could express! As he watched | 102 | _____
these Deaf he began to understand dimly some of the joy they felt | 115 | _____
in their arrival at the perfect meaning, the exact word, the shade | 127 | _____
of difference between "discipline" and "punishment," between | 134 | _____
"respectful" and "respectable." He had begun to try to read the | 145 | _____
newspaper and later had even bought a dictionary by which he | 156 | _____
hoped to be made able to understand it. Janice had laughed at | 168 | _____
him and accused him of trying to make himself more than he was, | 181 | _____
and later of using his reading to close away her advice. Both of | 194 | _____
these things were true, but it was also true that over the years, | 207 | _____
Abel's world had widened more than hers. | 214 | _____

Needs Work   1 2 3 4 5   Excellent
        Paid attention to punctuation

Needs Work   1 2 3 4 5   Excellent
            Sounded good

Total Words Read _____

Total Errors − _____

Correct WPM _____

55

Fiction

from *In This Sign*

by Joanne Greenberg

Discover that finding the perfect meaning of words can widen
your understanding of the world.

	Words Read	Miscues

The newspaper had been an affectation at first, and a defense — 11

against having to stare at people on the bus, but since [Abel] had — 24

come to be a leader in the Deaf community and someone to be — 37

consulted, he had come to know the few well-educated Deaf, in — 48

the city, people who spelled more than they Signed because their — 59

needs and knowledges exceeded the Signs that were used for the — 70

basic things of living. More and more he felt himself needing to — 82

grow into these new words. How complicated they were! How — 92

minutely subtle the differences they could express! As he watched — 102

these Deaf he began to understand dimly some of the joy they felt — 115

in their arrival at the perfect meaning, the exact word, the shade — 127

of difference between "discipline" and "punishment," between — 134

"respectful" and "respectable." He had begun to try to read the — 145

newspaper and later had even bought a dictionary by which he — 156

hoped to be made able to understand it. Janice had laughed at — 168

him and accused him of trying to make himself more than he was, — 181

and later of using his reading to close away her advice. Both of — 194

these things were true, but it was also true that over the years, — 207

Abel's world had widened more than hers. — 214

Needs Work 1 2 3 4 5 Excellent
Paid attention to punctuation

Needs Work 1 2 3 4 5 Excellent
Sounded good

Total Words Read _____

Total Errors − _____

Correct WPM _____

56 The Man Behind the Words

Nonfiction

Learn how J. Terry Edmonds's jump into politics made him a trailblazer.

First Reading

	Words Read	Miscues

When people hear a president speak, they rarely think about 　10 　_____

others helping to shape the presentation. Today, however, 　18 　_____

presidents depend on writers such as J. Terry Edmonds to help 　29 　_____

them communicate effectively. Edmonds is the first African 　37 　_____

American ever to work as a full-time speechwriter for a U.S. 　48 　_____

president; he is also the first African American to serve as director 　60 　_____

of speechwriting for the White House. His is an all-American 　70 　_____

story of success. 　73 　_____

　　Edmonds grew up in Baltimore, Maryland; his father drove a 　83 　_____

truck, and his mother worked as a waitress. A voracious reader, 　94 　_____

Edmonds demonstrated a gift for writing at his high school, 　104 　_____

Baltimore City College. After graduating in 1967, Edmonds went 　113 　_____

on to Morgan State University. 　118 　_____

　　Edmonds began his career in business, with jobs in public 　128 　_____

relations and communications. He joined the world of politics as 　138 　_____

press secretary for his congressman from Baltimore. During 　146 　_____

President Bill Clinton's administration, he wrote speeches for 　154 　_____

Health and Human Services Secretary Donna Shalala and worked 　163 　_____

in a number of jobs in the White House and in federal offices. 　176 　_____

President Clinton then appointed him to the office of director of 　187 　_____

speechwriting. Following the 2000 elections, Edmonds returned 　194 　_____

to Morgan State University as the school's special assistant to the 　205 　_____

president for 2001–2002. 　209 　_____

Needs Work　1　2　3　4　5　Excellent
　　　Paid attention to punctuation

Needs Work　1　2　3　4　5　Excellent
　　　Sounded good

Total Words Read _____

Total Errors − _____

Correct WPM _____

111

The Man Behind the Words

Learn how J. Terry Edmonds's jump into politics made him a trailblazer.

	Words Read	Miscues
When people hear a president speak, they rarely think about	10	_____
others helping to shape the presentation. Today, however,	18	_____
presidents depend on writers such as J. Terry Edmonds to help	29	_____
them communicate effectively. Edmonds is the first African	37	_____
American ever to work as a full-time speechwriter for a U.S.	48	_____
president; he is also the first African American to serve as director	60	_____
of speechwriting for the White House. His is an all-American	70	_____
story of success.	73	_____
Edmonds grew up in Baltimore, Maryland; his father drove a	83	_____
truck, and his mother worked as a waitress. A voracious reader,	94	_____
Edmonds demonstrated a gift for writing at his high school,	104	_____
Baltimore City College. After graduating in 1967, Edmonds went	113	_____
on to Morgan State University.	118	_____
Edmonds began his career in business, with jobs in public	128	_____
relations and communications. He joined the world of politics as	138	_____
press secretary for his congressman from Baltimore. During	146	_____
President Bill Clinton's administration, he wrote speeches for	154	_____
Health and Human Services Secretary Donna Shalala and worked	163	_____
in a number of jobs in the White House and in federal offices.	176	_____
President Clinton then appointed him to the office of director of	187	_____
speechwriting. Following the 2000 elections, Edmonds returned	194	_____
to Morgan State University as the school's special assistant to the	205	_____
president for 2001–2002.	209	_____

Needs Work   1   2   3   4   5   Excellent
Paid attention to punctuation

Needs Work   1   2   3   4   5   Excellent
Sounded good

Total Words Read _____

Total Errors − _____

Correct WPM _____

57 from *Sense and Sensibility*

Fiction   by Jane Austen

Learn about the residents of the Dashwood estate in 19th-century
Victorian England.

First Reading

	Words Read	Miscues

The family of Dashwood had been long settled in Sussex. Their	11	_____
estate was large, and their residence was at Norland Park, in the	23	_____
center of their property, where for many generations they had	33	_____
lived in so respectable a manner as to engage the general good	45	_____
opinion of their surrounding acquaintance. The late owner of this	55	_____
estate was a single man, who lived to a very advanced age, and	68	_____
who for many years of his life had a constant companion and	80	_____
housekeeper in his sister. But her death, which happened ten	90	_____
years before his own, produced a great alteration in his home; for	102	_____
to supply her loss, he invited and received into his house the	114	_____
family of his nephew, Mr. Henry Dashwood, the legal inheritor of	125	_____
the Norland estate, and the person to whom he intended to	136	_____
bequeath it. In the society of his nephew and niece, and their	148	_____
children, the old gentleman's days were comfortably spent. His	157	_____
attachment to them all increased. The constant attention of Mr.	167	_____
and Mrs. Henry Dashwood to his wishes, which proceeded not	177	_____
merely from interest, but from goodness of heart, gave him every	188	_____
degree of solid comfort which his age could receive; and the	199	_____
cheerfulness of the children added a relish to his existence.	209	_____

Needs Work   1   2   3   4   5   Excellent
     Paid attention to punctuation

Needs Work   1   2   3   4   5   Excellent
     Sounded good

Total Words Read   _____

Total Errors   − _____

Correct WPM   _____

57

Fiction

from *Sense and Sensibility*
by Jane Austen

Learn about the residents of the Dashwood estate in 19th-century Victorian England.

	Words Read	Miscues
The family of Dashwood had been long settled in Sussex. Their	11	_____
estate was large, and their residence was at Norland Park, in the	23	_____
center of their property, where for many generations they had	33	_____
lived in so respectable a manner as to engage the general good	45	_____
opinion of their surrounding acquaintance. The late owner of this	55	_____
estate was a single man, who lived to a very advanced age, and	68	_____
who for many years of his life had a constant companion and	80	_____
housekeeper in his sister. But her death, which happened ten	90	_____
years before his own, produced a great alteration in his home; for	102	_____
to supply her loss, he invited and received into his house the	114	_____
family of his nephew, Mr. Henry Dashwood, the legal inheritor of	125	_____
the Norland estate, and the person to whom he intended to	136	_____
bequeath it. In the society of his nephew and niece, and their	148	_____
children, the old gentleman's days were comfortably spent. His	157	_____
attachment to them all increased. The constant attention of Mr.	167	_____
and Mrs. Henry Dashwood to his wishes, which proceeded not	177	_____
merely from interest, but from goodness of heart, gave him every	188	_____
degree of solid comfort which his age could receive; and the	199	_____
cheerfulness of the children added a relish to his existence.	209	_____

Needs Work   1   2   3   4   5   Excellent
Paid attention to punctuation

Needs Work   1   2   3   4   5   Excellent
Sounded good

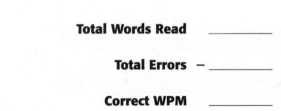

Total Words Read _____

Total Errors − _____

Correct WPM _____

58 from "The Enormous Radio"

Fiction by John Cheever

Read about a woman's bizarre experience with a wooden
1950s-era furniture-size hi-fi radio.

First Reading

	Words Read	Miscues

The radio was delivered at the kitchen door the following	10	_____
afternoon, and with the assistance of her maid and the handyman	21	_____
Irene uncrated it and brought it into the living room. She was	33	_____
struck at once with the physical ugliness of the large gumwood	44	_____
cabinet. Irene was proud of her living room, she had chosen its	56	_____
furnishings and colors as carefully as she chose her clothes, and	67	_____
now it seemed to her that the new radio stood among her	79	_____
intimate possessions like an aggressive intruder. She was	87	_____
confounded by the number of dials and switches on the	97	_____
instrument panel, and she studied them thoroughly before she	106	_____
put the plug into a wall socket and turned the radio on. The dials	120	_____
flooded with a malevolent green light, and in the distance she	131	_____
heard the music of a piano quintet. The quintet was in the	143	_____
distance for only an instant; it bore down upon her with a speed	156	_____
greater than light and filled the apartment with the noise of music	168	_____
amplified so mightily that it knocked a china ornament from a	179	_____
table to the floor. She rushed to the instrument and reduced the	191	_____
volume. The violent forces that were snared in the ugly gumwood	202	_____
cabinet made her uneasy.	206	_____

Needs Work   1 2 3 4 5   Excellent
_____
Paid attention to punctuation

Needs Work   1 2 3 4 5   Excellent
_____
Sounded good

Total Words Read _____

Total Errors −_____

Correct WPM _____

58

Fiction

from "The Enormous Radio"

by John Cheever

Read about a woman's bizarre experience with a wooden
1950s-era furniture-size hi-fi radio.

	Words Read	Miscues

The radio was delivered at the kitchen door the following	10	_____
afternoon, and with the assistance of her maid and the handyman	21	_____
Irene uncrated it and brought it into the living room. She was	33	_____
struck at once with the physical ugliness of the large gumwood	44	_____
cabinet. Irene was proud of her living room, she had chosen its	56	_____
furnishings and colors as carefully as she chose her clothes, and	67	_____
now it seemed to her that the new radio stood among her	79	_____
intimate possessions like an aggressive intruder. She was	87	_____
confounded by the number of dials and switches on the	97	_____
instrument panel, and she studied them thoroughly before she	106	_____
put the plug into a wall socket and turned the radio on. The dials	120	_____
flooded with a malevolent green light, and in the distance she	131	_____
heard the music of a piano quintet. The quintet was in the	143	_____
distance for only an instant; it bore down upon her with a speed	156	_____
greater than light and filled the apartment with the noise of music	168	_____
amplified so mightly that it knocked a china ornament from a	179	_____
table to the floor. She rushed to the instrument and reduced the	191	_____
volume. The violent forces that were snared in the ugly gumwood	202	_____
cabinet made her uneasy.	206	_____

Needs Work   1   2   3   4   5   Excellent
Paid attention to punctuation

Needs Work   1   2   3   4   5   Excellent
Sounded good

Total Words Read   _____

Total Errors – _____

Correct WPM   _____

59

Fiction

from *The War of the Worlds*

by H. G. Wells

Call upon your senses for this description of Martians invading Earth.

First Reading

	Words Read	Miscues

Each of the Martians, standing in the great crescent I have | 11 | _____

described, had discharged, by means of the gunlike tube he | 21 | _____

carried, a huge canister over whatever hill, copse, cluster of | 31 | _____

houses, or other possible cover for guns, chanced to be in front of | 44 | _____

him. Some fired only one of these, some two—as in the case of | 58 | _____

the one we had seen; the one at Ripley is said to have discharged | 72 | _____

no fewer than five at that time. These canisters smashed on | 83 | _____

striking the ground—they did not explode—and incontinently | 92 | _____

disengaged an enormous volume of heavy, inky vapor, coiling and | 102 | _____

pouring upward in a huge and ebony cumulus cloud, a gaseous | 113 | _____

hill that sank and spread itself slowly over the surrounding | 123 | _____

country. And the touch of that vapor, the inhaling of its pungent | 135 | _____

wisps, was death to all that breathes. | 142 | _____

It was heavy, this vapor, heavier than the densest smoke, so | 153 | _____

that, after the first tumultuous uprush and outflow of its impact, | 164 | _____

it sank down through the air and poured over the ground in a | 177 | _____

manner rather liquid than gaseous, abandoning the hills, and | 186 | _____

streaming into the valleys and ditches and watercourses even as | 196 | _____

I have heard the carbonic-acid gas that pours from volcanic clefts | 207 | _____

is wont to do. | 211 | _____

Needs Work   1   2   3   4   5   Excellent
Paid attention to punctuation

Needs Work   1   2   3   4   5   Excellent
Sounded good

Total Words Read _____

Total Errors − _____

Correct WPM _____

59 from *The War of the Worlds*

Fiction   by H. G. Wells

Call upon your senses for this description of Martians
invading Earth.

	Words Read	Miscues
Each of the Martians, standing in the great crescent I have	11	_____
described, had discharged, by means of the gunlike tube he	21	_____
carried, a huge canister over whatever hill, copse, cluster of	31	_____
houses, or other possible cover for guns, chanced to be in front of	44	_____
him. Some fired only one of these, some two—as in the case of	58	_____
the one we had seen; the one at Ripley is said to have discharged	72	_____
no fewer than five at that time. These canisters smashed on	83	_____
striking the ground—they did not explode—and incontinently	92	_____
disengaged an enormous volume of heavy, inky vapor, coiling and	102	_____
pouring upward in a huge and ebony cumulus cloud, a gaseous	113	_____
hill that sank and spread itself slowly over the surrounding	123	_____
country. And the touch of that vapor, the inhaling of its pungent	135	_____
wisps, was death to all that breathes.	142	_____
It was heavy, this vapor, heavier than the densest smoke, so	153	_____
that, after the first tumultuous uprush and outflow of its impact,	164	_____
it sank down through the air and poured over the ground in a	177	_____
manner rather liquid than gaseous, abandoning the hills, and	186	_____
streaming into the valleys and ditches and watercourses even as	196	_____
I have heard the carbonic-acid gas that pours from volcanic clefts	207	_____
is wont to do.	211	_____

Needs Work   1   2   3   4   5   Excellent
_____
         Paid attention to punctuation

Needs Work   1   2   3   4   5   Excellent
_____
         Sounded good

Total Words Read _____

Total Errors − _____

Correct WPM _____

60
Nonfiction

from *Tutankhamun:*
The Untold Story
by Thomas Hoving

Imagine the archaeologist's excitement as he literally stands on the threshold of a major discovery.

First Reading

	Words Read	Miscues

The royal seal showed that the tomb had at least been used for a — 14 _____

person of very noble standing. And whatever lay beyond had not — 25 _____

been entered since the end of the Twentieth Dynasty—three — 35 _____

thousand years before—since the door had been completely — 44 _____

covered up by the workers' huts of Ramesses VI. — 53 _____

While examining the seals, Carter had noticed, at the very top — 64 _____

of the doorway where some plaster had dropped down, a heavy — 75 _____

wooden lintel. Just under the beam of wood he made a small — 87 _____

hole barely large enough to peer through with a flashlight. The — 98 _____

space beyond the door was filled completely with stones and — 108 _____

rubble, further proof of the great care with which the tomb had — 120 _____

been protected. — 122 _____

It was, for Howard Carter, the most thrilling moment in his — 133 _____

long career. There he was, alone, except for his Arab workmen, on — 145 _____

the verge of what might be a unique discovery in the history of — 156 _____

Egyptian archaeology. In that blocked passage—beyond it in a — 168 _____

host of chambers—could be unimaginable treasures, unbelievable — 176 _____

discoveries. Carter had to hold himself in check with all the — 187 _____

professional discipline he could muster to prevent himself from — 196 _____

smashing the doorway and entering into the enticing and — 205 _____

mysterious space. — 207 _____

Needs Work   1   2   3   4   5   Excellent
Paid attention to punctuation

Needs Work   1   2   3   4   5   Excellent
Sounded good

Total Words Read _____

Total Errors − _____

Correct WPM _____

from *Tutankhamun:*

The Untold Story

by Thomas Hoving

Imagine the archaeologist's excitement as he literally stands on the threshold of a major discovery.

Second Reading

	Words Read	Miscues

The royal seal showed that the tomb had at least been used for a | 14 | _____

person of very noble standing. And whatever lay beyond had not | 25 | _____

been entered since the end of the Twentieth Dynasty—three | 35 | _____

thousand years before—since the door had been completely | 44 | _____

covered up by the workers' huts of Ramesses VI. | 53 | _____

While examining the seals, Carter had noticed, at the very top | 64 | _____

of the doorway where some plaster had dropped down, a heavy | 75 | _____

wooden lintel. Just under the beam of wood he made a small | 87 | _____

hole barely large enough to peer through with a flashlight. The | 98 | _____

space beyond the door was filled completely with stones and | 108 | _____

rubble, further proof of the great care with which the tomb had | 120 | _____

been protected. | 122 | _____

It was, for Howard Carter, the most thrilling moment in his | 133 | _____

long career. There he was, alone, except for his Arab workmen, on | 145 | _____

the verge of what might be a unique discovery in the history of | 156 | _____

Egyptian archaeology. In that blocked passage—beyond it in a | 168 | _____

host of chambers—could be unimaginable treasures, unbelievable | 176 | _____

discoveries. Carter had to hold himself in check with all the | 187 | _____

professional discipline he could muster to prevent himself from | 196 | _____

smashing the doorway and entering into the enticing and | 205 | _____

mysterious space. | 207 | _____

Needs Work   1   2   3   4   5   Excellent
Paid attention to punctuation

Needs Work   1   2   3   4   5   Excellent
Sounded good

Total Words Read _____

Total Errors − _____

Correct WPM _____

61 Kublai Khan

Nonfiction

Learn about the conqueror of China who also was a tolerant and insightful ruler.

	Words Read	Miscues
First Reading		

	Words Read	Miscues
Kublai Khan lived from 1215 to 1294. He was the grandson	11	_____
of Genghis Khan, who had established the Mongol empire. Like	21	_____
his grandfather, Kublai Khan was an emperor and a conqueror.	31	_____
He became ruler of the Mongol empire in 1260. During his reign,	43	_____
the Mongol empire reached its largest size, stretching from	52	_____
eastern Europe to eastern Asia. After conquering China, Kublai	61	_____
Khan established the Yuan dynasty, which lasted from 1279 to	71	_____
1368. The Yuan dynasty marked the first time that foreigners	81	_____
ruled China.	83	_____
Kublai Khan ruled his empire from China rather than from	93	_____
Mongolia. Tolerant of most religious beliefs, he built schools,	102	_____
wrote new laws, reduced taxes, promoted trade, and used a	112	_____
pony-express-style message-relay system. He also ordered the	119	_____
construction of a new capital city, Daidu, which today is part of	131	_____
the Chinese capital of Beijing. Although he had Chinese advisors,	141	_____
the emperor distrusted the Chinese, perhaps because they had	150	_____
been enemies of the Mongols for many years. Therefore, he	160	_____
appointed Mongolians to top government positions and recruited	168	_____
foreigners to help govern his vast realm.	175	_____
Although Kublai Khan twice tried to invade Japan, his efforts	185	_____
to expand the Mongol empire farther eastward failed. Instead, he	195	_____
focused his attention on maintaining his empire.	202	_____

Needs Work   1   2   3   4   5   Excellent
Paid attention to punctuation

Needs Work   1   2   3   4   5   Excellent
Sounded good

Total Words Read _____

Total Errors − _____

Correct WPM _____

61 Kublai Khan

Nonfiction

Learn about the conqueror of China who also was a tolerant and insightful ruler.

Second Reading

	Words Read	Miscues

Kublai Khan lived from 1215 to 1294. He was the grandson | 11 | _____
of Genghis Khan, who had established the Mongol empire. Like | 21 | _____
his grandfather, Kublai Khan was an emperor and a conqueror. | 31 | _____
He became ruler of the Mongol empire in 1260. During his reign, | 43 | _____
the Mongol empire reached its largest size, stretching from | 52 | _____
eastern Europe to eastern Asia. After conquering China, Kublai | 61 | _____
Khan established the Yuan dynasty, which lasted from 1279 to | 71 | _____
1368. The Yuan dynasty marked the first time that foreigners | 81 | _____
ruled China. | 83 | _____

Kublai Khan ruled his empire from China rather than from | 93 | _____
Mongolia. Tolerant of most religious beliefs, he built schools, | 102 | _____
wrote new laws, reduced taxes, promoted trade, and used a | 112 | _____
pony-express-style message-relay system. He also ordered the | 119 | _____
construction of a new capital city, Daidu, which today is part of | 131 | _____
the Chinese capital of Beijing. Although he had Chinese advisors, | 141 | _____
the emperor distrusted the Chinese, perhaps because they had | 150 | _____
been enemies of the Mongols for many years. Therefore, he | 160 | _____
appointed Mongolians to top government positions and recruited | 168 | _____
foreigners to help govern his vast realm. | 175 | _____

Although Kublai Khan twice tried to invade Japan, his efforts | 185 | _____
to expand the Mongol empire farther eastward failed. Instead, he | 195 | _____
focused his attention on maintaining his empire. | 202 | _____

Needs Work   1   2   3   4   5   Excellent
Paid attention to punctuation

Needs Work   1   2   3   4   5   Excellent
Sounded good

Total Words Read _____

Total Errors − _____

Correct WPM _____

62

Nonfiction

from *Up from Slavery*

by Booker T. Washington

Discover how enslaved persons made themselves aware of the events and the effects of the Civil War.

First Reading

	Words Read	Miscues

From the time that Garrison, Lovejoy, and others began to agitate | 11 | _____

for freedom, the slaves throughout the South kept in close touch | 22 | _____

with the progress of the movement. Though I was a mere child | 34 | _____

during the preparation for the Civil War and during the war itself, | 46 | _____

I now recall the many late-at-night whispered discussions that I | 56 | _____

heard my mother and the other slaves on the plantation indulge | 67 | _____

in. These discussions showed that they understood the situation, | 76 | _____

and that they kept themselves informed of events by what was | 87 | _____

termed the "grape-vine" telegraph. | 91 | _____

During the campaign when Lincoln was first a candidate for | 101 | _____

the Presidency, the slaves on our far-off plantation, miles from any | 112 | _____

railroad or large city or daily newspaper, knew what the issues | 123 | _____

involved were. When war was begun between the North and the | 134 | _____

South, every slave on our plantation felt and knew that, though | 145 | _____

other issues were discussed, the primal one was that of slavery. | 156 | _____

Even the most ignorant members of my race on the remote | 167 | _____

plantations felt in their hearts, with a certainty that admitted of | 178 | _____

no doubt, that the freedom of the slaves would be the one great | 191 | _____

result of the war, if the Northern armies conquered. | 200 | _____

Needs Work   1   2   3   4   5   Excellent
Paid attention to punctuation

Needs Work   1   2   3   4   5   Excellent
Sounded good

Total Words Read _____

Total Errors − _____

Correct WPM _____

from *Up from Slavery*
by Booker T. Washington

Discover how enslaved persons made themselves aware of the
events and the effects of the Civil War.

From the time that Garrison, Lovejoy, and others began to agitate	11	_____
for freedom, the slaves throughout the South kept in close touch	22	_____
with the progress of the movement. Though I was a mere child	34	_____
during the preparation for the Civil War and during the war itself,	46	_____
I now recall the many late-at-night whispered discussions that I	56	_____
heard my mother and the other slaves on the plantation indulge	67	_____
in. These discussions showed that they understood the situation,	76	_____
and that they kept themselves informed of events by what was	87	_____
termed the "grape-vine" telegraph.	91	_____
During the campaign when Lincoln was first a candidate for	101	_____
the Presidency, the slaves on our far-off plantation, miles from any	112	_____
railroad or large city or daily newspaper, knew what the issues	123	_____
involved were. When war was begun between the North and the	134	_____
South, every slave on our plantation felt and knew that, though	145	_____
other issues were discussed, the primal one was that of slavery.	156	_____
Even the most ignorant members of my race on the remote	167	_____
plantations felt in their hearts, with a certainty that admitted of	178	_____
no doubt, that the freedom of the slaves would be the one great	191	_____
result of the war, if the Northern armies conquered.	200	_____

Needs Work   1 2 3 4 5   Excellent
> *Paid attention to punctuation*

Needs Work   1 2 3 4 5   Excellent
> *Sounded good*

Total Words Read _____

Total Errors − _____

Correct WPM _____

63
Fiction

from *In the Name of Salomé*
by Julia Alvarez

Stand in the wings with reluctant Camilla as she waits to give
a speech about her famous mother.

First Reading

	Words Read	Miscues

This is her first public pronouncement as a member of her | 11 | _____

famous family. She has been surprised to receive so many | 21 | _____

invitations to speak about her mother this year. She is, after all, | 33 | _____

the anonymous one, the one who has done nothing remarkable. | 43 | _____

But—and this annoys her—she is in demand for sentimental | 54 | _____

reasons, the daughter who lost her mother, the orphan marched | 64 | _____

out in her starched party dress to recite her mother's poem, "El | 76 | _____

ave y el nido," to the sobs of old aunts and family friends. | 89 | _____

Perhaps that is precisely what she should do, throw away this | 100 | _____

uninspiring hour she has typed onto twenty pages—a review of | 111 | _____

the history of Hispaniola, Gallego, and Quintana as prosodic | 120 | _____

influences on her mother's patriotic poems, her mother's | 128 | _____

pseudonym, . . . one short anecdote about a jealous rival stealing | 137 | _____

her mother's pseudonym thrown in like the rattle one shakes at a | 149 | _____

fussy child to distract it from bursting out in shrieks in front of | 162 | _____

company one is trying to impress. And instead, put on her | 173 | _____

mother's black dress, hang the beribboned national medal over | 182 | _____

her head, and come out in a spotlight like a butterfly pinned to | 195 | _____

a swatch of bright fabric, and recite the old favorites. | 205 | _____

Needs Work   1   2   3   4   5   Excellent
Paid attention to punctuation

Needs Work   1   2   3   4   5   Excellent
Sounded good

Total Words Read _____

Total Errors − _____

Correct WPM _____

63

Fiction

from *In the Name of Salomé*

by Julia Alvarez

Stand in the wings with reluctant Camilla as she waits to give
a speech about her famous mother.

This is her first public pronouncement as a member of her	11	_____
famous family. She has been surprised to receive so many	21	_____
invitations to speak about her mother this year. She is, after all,	33	_____
the anonymous one, the one who has done nothing remarkable.	43	_____
But—and this annoys her—she is in demand for sentimental	54	_____
reasons, the daughter who lost her mother, the orphan marched	64	_____
out in her starched party dress to recite her mother's poem, "El	76	_____
ave y el nido," to the sobs of old aunts and family friends.	89	_____
Perhaps that is precisely what she should do, throw away this	100	_____
uninspiring hour she has typed onto twenty pages—a review of	111	_____
the history of Hispaniola, Gallego, and Quintana as prosodic	120	_____
influences on her mother's patriotic poems, her mother's	128	_____
pseudonym, . . . one short anecdote about a jealous rival stealing	137	_____
her mother's pseudonym thrown in like the rattle one shakes at a	149	_____
fussy child to distract it from bursting out in shrieks in front of	162	_____
company one is trying to impress. And instead, put on her	173	_____
mother's black dress, hang the beribboned national medal over	182	_____
her head, and come out in a spotlight like a butterfly pinned to	195	_____
a swatch of bright fabric, and recite the old favorites.	205	_____

Needs Work   1   2   3   4   5   Excellent
       Paid attention to punctuation

Needs Work   1   2   3   4   5   Excellent
       Sounded good

Total Words Read _____

Total Errors − _____

Correct WPM _____

64
Fiction

from "The Lottery"
by Shirley Jackson

Look for clues that indicate that something terrible is going to happen in this story.

	Words Read	Miscues

The morning of June 27th was clear and sunny, with the fresh | 12 | _____

warmth of a full-summer day; the flowers were blossoming | 21 | _____

profusely and the grass was richly green. The people of the village | 33 | _____

began to gather in the square, between the post office and the | 45 | _____

bank, around ten o'clock; in some towns there were so many | 56 | _____

people that the lottery took two days and had to be started on | 69 | _____

June 26th, but in this village, where there were only about three | 81 | _____

hundred people, the whole lottery took less than two hours, so it | 93 | _____

could begin at ten o'clock in the morning and still be through in | 106 | _____

time to allow the villagers to get home for noon dinner. | 117 | _____

The children assembled first, of course. School was recently | 126 | _____

over for the summer, and the feeling of liberty sat uneasily on | 138 | _____

most of them; they tended to gather together quietly for a while | 150 | _____

before they broke into boisterous play, and their talk was still of | 162 | _____

the classroom and the teacher, of books and reprimands. Bobby | 172 | _____

Martin had already stuffed his pockets full of stones, and the | 183 | _____

other boys soon followed his example, selecting the smoothest | 192 | _____

and roundest stones; Bobby and Harry Jones and Dickie | 201 | _____

Delacroix—the villagers pronounced his name "Dellacroy"— | 208 | _____

eventually made a great pile of stones in one corner of the square. | 221 | _____

Needs Work   1 2 3 4 5   Excellent
Paid attention to punctuation

Needs Work   1 2 3 4 5   Excellent
Sounded good

Total Words Read _____

Total Errors − _____

Correct WPM _____

64

Fiction

from "The Lottery"

by Shirley Jackson

Look for clues that indicate that something terrible is going to happen in this story.

	Words Read	Miscues
The morning of June 27th was clear and sunny, with the fresh	12	_____
warmth of a full-summer day; the flowers were blossoming	21	_____
profusely and the grass was richly green. The people of the village	33	_____
began to gather in the square, between the post office and the	45	_____
bank, around ten o'clock; in some towns there were so many	56	_____
people that the lottery took two days and had to be started on	69	_____
June 26th, but in this village, where there were only about three	81	_____
hundred people, the whole lottery took less than two hours, so it	93	_____
could begin at ten o'clock in the morning and still be through in	106	_____
time to allow the villagers to get home for noon dinner.	117	_____
The children assembled first, of course. School was recently	126	_____
over for the summer, and the feeling of liberty sat uneasily on	138	_____
most of them; they tended to gather together quietly for a while	150	_____
before they broke into boisterous play, and their talk was still of	162	_____
the classroom and the teacher, of books and reprimands. Bobby	172	_____
Martin had already stuffed his pockets full of stones, and the	183	_____
other boys soon followed his example, selecting the smoothest	192	_____
and roundest stones; Bobby and Harry Jones and Dickie	201	_____
Delacroix—the villagers pronounced his name "Dellacroy"—	208	_____
eventually made a great pile of stones in one corner of the square.	221	_____

Needs Work   1   2   3   4   5   Excellent
Paid attention to punctuation

Needs Work   1   2   3   4   5   Excellent
Sounded good

Total Words Read _____

Total Errors – _____

Correct WPM _____

65
Nonfiction

from *Pack of Two:*
The Intricate Bond Between People and Dogs
by Caroline Knapp

Consider your own feelings about dogs while you read from this
unique relationship study.

First Reading

	Words Read	Miscues

Before you get a dog, you can't quite imagine what living with | 12 | _____
one might be like; afterward, you can't imagine living any other | 23 | _____
way. Life without Lucille? Unfathomable, to contemplate how | 31 | _____
quiet and still my home would be, and how much less laughter | 43 | _____
there'd be, and how much less tenderness, and how unanchored | 53 | _____
I'd feel without her presence, the simple constancy of it. I once | 65 | _____
heard a woman who'd lost her dog say that she felt as though a | 79 | _____
color were suddenly missing from her world: the dog had | 89 | _____
introduced to her field of vision some previously unavailable hue, | 99 | _____
and without the dog, that color was gone. That seemed to | 110 | _____
capture the experience of loving a dog with eminent simplicity. | 120 | _____
I'd amend it only slightly and say that if we are open to what they | 135 | _____
have to give us, dogs can introduce us to several colors, with | 147 | _____
names like wildness and nurturance and trust and joy. | 156 | _____

I am not sentimental about dogs, my passion for Lucille | 166 | _____
notwithstanding. I don't share the view, popular among some | 175 | _____
animal aficionados, that dogs are necessarily higher beings, that | 184 | _____
they represent a canine version of shamans, capable by virtue of | 195 | _____
their wild ancestry or nobility of offering humans a particular | 205 | _____
kind of wisdom or healing. | 210 | _____

Needs Work   1   2   3   4   5   Excellent
Paid attention to punctuation

Needs Work   1   2   3   4   5   Excellent
Sounded good

Total Words Read _____

Total Errors − _____

Correct WPM _____

from *Pack of Two:*

The Intricate Bond Between People and Dogs

by Caroline Knapp

Consider your own feelings about dogs while you read from this unique relationship study.

	Words Read	Miscues
Before you get a dog, you can't quite imagine what living with	12	_____
one might be like; afterward, you can't imagine living any other	23	_____
way. Life without Lucille? Unfathomable, to contemplate how	31	_____
quiet and still my home would be, and how much less laughter	43	_____
there'd be, and how much less tenderness, and how unanchored	53	_____
I'd feel without her presence, the simple constancy of it. I once	65	_____
heard a woman who'd lost her dog say that she felt as though a	79	_____
color were suddenly missing from her world: the dog had	89	_____
introduced to her field of vision some previously unavailable hue,	99	_____
and without the dog, that color was gone. That seemed to	110	_____
capture the experience of loving a dog with eminent simplicity.	120	_____
I'd amend it only slightly and say that if we are open to what they	135	_____
have to give us, dogs can introduce us to several colors, with	147	_____
names like wildness and nurturance and trust and joy.	156	_____
I am not sentimental about dogs, my passion for Lucille	166	_____
notwithstanding. I don't share the view, popular among some	175	_____
animal aficionados, that dogs are necessarily higher beings, that	184	_____
they represent a canine version of shamans, capable by virtue of	195	_____
their wild ancestry or nobility of offering humans a particular	205	_____
kind of wisdom or healing.	210	_____

Needs Work   1   2   3   4   5   Excellent
Paid attention to punctuation

Needs Work   1   2   3   4   5   Excellent
Sounded good

Total Words Read _____

Total Errors − _____

Correct WPM _____

66

Nonfiction

from *Open Net*
by George Plimpton

Discover how the author prepares to become a goalie for a
professional hockey team.

〰〰〰

	Words Read	Miscues

While my evenings were taken up with skating sessions at the | 11 | _____ |
Skyrink, I prepared for Fitchburg in more sedentary ways. I did | 22 | _____ |
considerable reading—instruction manuals (especially on | 28 | _____ |
goaltending) and various biographies of hockey personalities. I | 36 | _____ |
kept notes. Also I thought a lot about the protective face mask I | 49 | _____ |
had bought at Cosby's. My notion was to get it decorated in such | 62 | _____ |
a way that would perhaps give the opposition a slight start, as well | 75 | _____ |
as providing me with a small psychological boost. | 83 | _____ |

The face mask has been around since November 2, 1959 (I | 94 | _____ |
wondered if I ever would have had the nerve to accept playing in | 107 | _____ |
the goal if such things were not available), when the Montreal | 118 | _____ |
Canadiens' Jacques Plante introduced his in a game against the | 128 | _____ |
New York Rangers in New York's Madison Square Garden. Plante | 138 | _____ |
had a wonderful excuse: "I already had four broken noses, a | 149 | _____ |
broken jaw, two broken cheekbones, and almost 200 stitches in | 159 | _____ |
my head. I didn't care how the mask looked. I was afraid I would | 173 | _____ |
look just like the mask, the way things were going." Incredibly, his | 185 | _____ |
colleagues looked upon Plante with scorn for wearing such a | 195 | _____ |
thing—derisive comments were made that he had gone soft. | 205 | _____ |

Needs Work 1 2 3 4 5 Excellent
Paid attention to punctuation

Needs Work 1 2 3 4 5 Excellent
Sounded good

Total Words Read _____

Total Errors − _____

Correct WPM _____

from *Open Net*

by George Plimpton

Discover how the author prepares to become a goalie for a professional hockey team.

	Words Read	Miscues
While my evenings were taken up with skating sessions at the	11	_____
Skyrink, I prepared for Fitchburg in more sedentary ways. I did	22	_____
considerable reading—instruction manuals (especially on	28	_____
goaltending) and various biographies of hockey personalities. I	36	_____
kept notes. Also I thought a lot about the protective face mask I	49	_____
had bought at Cosby's. My notion was to get it decorated in such	62	_____
a way that would perhaps give the opposition a slight start, as well	75	_____
as providing me with a small psychological boost.	83	_____
The face mask has been around since November 2, 1959 (I	94	_____
wondered if I ever would have had the nerve to accept playing in	107	_____
the goal if such things were not available), when the Montreal	118	_____
Canadiens' Jacques Plante introduced his in a game against the	128	_____
New York Rangers in New York's Madison Square Garden. Plante	138	_____
had a wonderful excuse: "I already had four broken noses, a	149	_____
broken jaw, two broken cheekbones, and almost 200 stitches in	159	_____
my head. I didn't care how the mask looked. I was afraid I would	173	_____
look just like the mask, the way things were going." Incredibly, his	185	_____
colleagues looked upon Plante with scorn for wearing such a	195	_____
thing—derisive comments were made that he had gone soft.	205	_____

Needs Work   1   2   3   4   5   Excellent

Paid attention to punctuation

Needs Work   1   2   3   4   5   Excellent

Sounded good

Total Words Read   _____

Total Errors   − _____

Correct WPM   _____

67

Fiction

from *Time and Again*

by Jack Finney

Picture the stone and metal and glass towers of New York's famous Fifth Avenue.

	Words Read	Miscues
I looked at Kate and she was grinning; then I turned to look	13	_____
south, down the long familiar length of Fifth Avenue, and once	24	_____
more the faintness touched me.	29	_____
Everyone has seen in actuality or on film the splendid	39	_____
glittering length of Fifth Avenue, the wide wide street solidly lined	50	_____
with incredible towers of metal, glass, and soaring stone: the	60	_____
sparkling Corning Glass Building, its acres of glass walls rising	70	_____
forever; the enormous aluminum-sided Tishman Building; the	77	_____
great stone masses of Rockefeller Center; weather-worn	84	_____
St. Patrick's Cathedral, its twin spires submerged down among the	94	_____
huge buildings which dwarf it. And the sparkling stores: Saks,	104	_____
Tiffany's, Jensen's; and the big, old soiled-white library at the	114	_____
corner of Forty-second Street, its stone lions flanking the wide	124	_____
steps of its main entrance. They must be the most famous	135	_____
seventeen blocks of the world, and beyond them even farther	145	_____
down the length of that astonishing street, the unbelievable height	155	_____
of the Empire State Building at Thirty-fourth Street, if the air	166	_____
should happen to be miraculously clear enough to see it. That was	178	_____
the picture—asphalt and stone and sky-touching towers of metal	188	_____
and glass—that was in my mind instinctively as I turned to look	201	_____
down the length of that street.	207	_____

Needs Work   1   2   3   4   5   Excellent
_____
Paid attention to punctuation

Needs Work   1   2   3   4   5   Excellent
_____
Sounded good

Total Words Read   _____

Total Errors − _____

Correct WPM   _____

from *Time and Again*

by Jack Finney

Picture the stone and metal and glass towers of New York's
famous Fifth Avenue.

	Words Read	Miscues
I looked at Kate and she was grinning; then I turned to look	13	_____
south, down the long familiar length of Fifth Avenue, and once	24	_____
more the faintness touched me.	29	_____
Everyone has seen in actuality or on film the splendid	39	_____
glittering length of Fifth Avenue, the wide wide street solidly lined	50	_____
with incredible towers of metal, glass, and soaring stone: the	60	_____
sparkling Corning Glass Building, its acres of glass walls rising	70	_____
forever; the enormous aluminum-sided Tishman Building; the	77	_____
great stone masses of Rockefeller Center; weather-worn	84	_____
St. Patrick's Cathedral, its twin spires submerged down among the	94	_____
huge buildings which dwarf it. And the sparkling stores: Saks,	104	_____
Tiffany's, Jensen's; and the big, old soiled-white library at the	114	_____
corner of Forty-second Street, its stone lions flanking the wide	124	_____
steps of its main entrance. They must be the most famous	135	_____
seventeen blocks of the world, and beyond them even farther	145	_____
down the length of that astonishing street, the unbelievable height	155	_____
of the Empire State Building at Thirty-fourth Street, if the air	166	_____
should happen to be miraculously clear enough to see it. That was	178	_____
the picture—asphalt and stone and sky-touching towers of metal	188	_____
and glass—that was in my mind instinctively as I turned to look	201	_____
down the length of that street.	207	_____

Needs Work   1   2   3   4   5   Excellent
Paid attention to punctuation

Needs Work   1   2   3   4   5   Excellent
Sounded good

Total Words Read   _____

Total Errors −_____

Correct WPM   _____

68 from *Wuthering Heights*

Fiction   by Emily Brontë

Imagine you are on the threshold of a Gothic mansion, and the
clouds are gathering.

	Words Read	Miscues
Wuthering Heights is the name of Mr. Heathcliff's dwelling.	9	_____
"Wuthering" being a significant provincial adjective descriptive of	17	_____
the atmospheric tumult to which its station is exposed in stormy	28	_____
weather. Pure, bracing ventilation they must have up there at all	39	_____
times, indeed: one may guess the power of the north wind	50	_____
blowing over the edge by the excessive slant of a few stunted firs	63	_____
at the end of the house; and by a range of gaunt thorns all	77	_____
stretching their limbs one way, as if craving alms of the sun.	89	_____
Happily, the architect had foresight to build it strong: the narrow	100	_____
windows are deeply set in the wall, and the corners defended with	112	_____
large jutting stones.	115	_____
Before passing the threshold, I paused to admire a quantity of	126	_____
grotesque carvings lavished over the front, and especially about	135	_____
the principal door; above which, among a wilderness of crumbling	145	_____
griffins, . . . I detected the date "1500," and the name "Hareton	155	_____
Earnshaw." I would have made a few comments and requested a	166	_____
short history of the place from the surly owner; but his attitude at	179	_____
the door appeared to demand my speedy entrance, or complete	189	_____
departure, and I had no desire to aggravate his impatience.	199	_____

Needs Work   1 2 3 4 5   Excellent
_____
Paid attention to punctuation

Needs Work   1 2 3 4 5   Excellent
_____
Sounded good

Total Words Read   _____

Total Errors − _____

Correct WPM   _____

68 Fiction from ***Wuthering Heights***

by Emily Brontë

Imagine you are on the threshold of a Gothic mansion, and the clouds are gathering.

	Words Read	Miscues

Wuthering Heights is the name of Mr. Heathcliff's dwelling. — 9 — ____

"Wuthering" being a significant provincial adjective descriptive of — 17 — ____

the atmospheric tumult to which its station is exposed in stormy — 28 — ____

weather. Pure, bracing ventilation they must have up there at all — 39 — ____

times, indeed: one may guess the power of the north wind — 50 — ____

blowing over the edge by the excessive slant of a few stunted firs — 63 — ____

at the end of the house; and by a range of gaunt thorns all — 77 — ____

stretching their limbs one way, as if craving alms of the sun. — 89 — ____

Happily, the architect had foresight to build it strong: the narrow — 100 — ____

windows are deeply set in the wall, and the corners defended with — 112 — ____

large jutting stones. — 115 — ____

Before passing the threshold, I paused to admire a quantity of — 126 — ____

grotesque carvings lavished over the front, and especially about — 135 — ____

the principal door; above which, among a wilderness of crumbling — 145 — ____

griffins, . . . I detected the date "1500," and the name "Hareton — 155 — ____

Earnshaw." I would have made a few comments and requested a — 166 — ____

short history of the place from the surly owner; but his attitude at — 179 — ____

the door appeared to demand my speedy entrance, or complete — 189 — ____

departure, and I had no desire to aggravate his impatience. — 199 — ____

Needs Work 1 2 3 4 5 Excellent
Paid attention to punctuation

Needs Work 1 2 3 4 5 Excellent
Sounded good

Total Words Read _____

Total Errors − _____

Correct WPM _____

69

Fiction

from *Little Women*
by Louisa May Alcott

Read about the daydreams of a young boy as he waits for the
March girls next door.

First Reading

	Words Read	Miscues

Laurie lay luxuriously swinging to and fro in his hammock one | 11 | _____

warm September afternoon, wondering what his neighbors were | 19 | _____

about, but too lazy to go and find out. He was in one of his | 34 | _____

moods; for the day had been both unprofitable and unsatisfactory, | 44 | _____

and he was wishing he could live it over again. The hot weather | 57 | _____

made him indolent, and he had shirked his studies, tried Mr. | 68 | _____

Brooke's patience to the utmost, displeased his grandfather by | 77 | _____

practicing half the afternoon, frightened the maidservants half out | 86 | _____

of their wits by mischievously hinting that one of his dogs was | 98 | _____

going mad, and, after high words with the stableman about some | 109 | _____

fancied neglect of his horse, he had flung himself into his | 120 | _____

hammock, to fume over the stupidity of the world in general, till | 132 | _____

the peace of the lovely day quieted him in spite of himself. Staring | 145 | _____

up into the green gloom of the horse-chestnut trees above him, he | 157 | _____

dreamed dreams of all sorts, and was just imagining himself | 167 | _____

tossing on the ocean, in a voyage round the world, when the | 179 | _____

sound of voices brought him ashore in a flash. Peeping through | 190 | _____

the meshes of his hammock, he saw the Marches coming out, as if | 203 | _____

bound on some expedition. | 207 | _____

Needs Work   1   2   3   4   5   Excellent
Paid attention to punctuation

Needs Work   1   2   3   4   5   Excellent
Sounded good

Total Words Read   _____

Total Errors   − _____

Correct WPM   _____

69

Fiction

from *Little Women*

by Louisa May Alcott

Read about the daydreams of a young boy as he waits for the
March girls next door.

	Words Read	Miscues
Laurie lay luxuriously swinging to and fro in his hammock one	11	_____
warm September afternoon, wondering what his neighbors were	19	_____
about, but too lazy to go and find out. He was in one of his	34	_____
moods; for the day had been both unprofitable and unsatisfactory,	44	_____
and he was wishing he could live it over again. The hot weather	57	_____
made him indolent, and he had shirked his studies, tried Mr.	68	_____
Brooke's patience to the utmost, displeased his grandfather by	77	_____
practicing half the afternoon, frightened the maidservants half out	86	_____
of their wits by mischievously hinting that one of his dogs was	98	_____
going mad, and, after high words with the stableman about some	109	_____
fancied neglect of his horse, he had flung himself into his	120	_____
hammock, to fume over the stupidity of the world in general, till	132	_____
the peace of the lovely day quieted him in spite of himself. Staring	145	_____
up into the green gloom of the horse-chestnut trees above him, he	157	_____
dreamed dreams of all sorts, and was just imagining himself	167	_____
tossing on the ocean, in a voyage round the world, when the	179	_____
sound of voices brought him ashore in a flash. Peeping through	190	_____
the meshes of his hammock, he saw the Marches coming out, as if	203	_____
bound on some expedition.	207	_____

Needs Work   1 2 3 4 5   Excellent
Paid attention to punctuation

Needs Work   1 2 3 4 5   Excellent
Sounded good

Total Words Read _____

Total Errors − _____

Correct WPM _____

70

Nonfiction

from *Having Our Say:*
The Delany Sisters' First 100 Years
by Sarah and A. Elizabeth Delany with Amy Hill Hearth

Learn about education options for blacks in the mid-1900s, as
told by two centenarians.

First Reading

	Words Read	Miscues
In the decades after the Civil War, "education" became the	10	_____
rallying cry of those seeking to improve the lot of former slaves,	22	_____
whose prospects were limited usually to hard labor in the fields or	34	_____
to domestic work in white people's homes. Black people during	44	_____
this era would be lucky to have had the chance to learn to read	58	_____
and write well enough to sign their own names.	67	_____
To the small but growing black middle class, it was clear that	79	_____
higher aspirations were unattainable without access to higher	87	_____
education. The few black students groomed for advancement	95	_____
found colleges and universities unwelcoming. Indeed, most	102	_____
institutions frankly barred them from admittance. Many white	110	_____
people clung to the belief that black people were incapable of	121	_____
being educated. In the black community, many argued that a	131	_____
classical education was a waste of time for people who had little	143	_____
hope of a future in which to use it. Black women faced even	156	_____
higher hurdles. At a time when most women were expected to	167	_____
marry and become mothers, higher education for them was	176	_____
deemed unnecessary.	178	_____
Black colleges were the crucial stepping-stone to progress,	186	_____
and they flourished. Northern philanthropists had established,	193	_____
among others, Howard University in Washington, D.C.	200	_____

Needs Work 1 2 3 4 5 Excellent
Paid attention to punctuation

Needs Work 1 2 3 4 5 Excellent
Sounded good

Total Words Read _____

Total Errors − _____

Correct WPM _____

139

from *Having Our Say:*

The Delany Sisters' First 100 Years

by Sarah and A. Elizabeth Delany with Amy Hill Hearth

Learn about education options for blacks in the mid-1900s, as
told by two centenarians.

In the decades after the Civil War, "education" became the	10
rallying cry of those seeking to improve the lot of former slaves,	22
whose prospects were limited usually to hard labor in the fields or	34
to domestic work in white people's homes. Black people during	44
this era would be lucky to have had the chance to learn to read	58
and write well enough to sign their own names.	67
To the small but growing black middle class, it was clear that	79
higher aspirations were unattainable without access to higher	87
education. The few black students groomed for advancement	95
found colleges and universities unwelcoming. Indeed, most	102
institutions frankly barred them from admittance. Many white	110
people clung to the belief that black people were incapable of	121
being educated. In the black community, many argued that a	131
classical education was a waste of time for people who had little	143
hope of a future in which to use it. Black women faced even	156
higher hurdles. At a time when most women were expected to	167
marry and become mothers, higher education for them was	176
deemed unnecessary.	178
Black colleges were the crucial stepping-stone to progress,	186
and they flourished. Northern philanthropists had established,	193
among others, Howard University in Washington, D.C.	200

Needs Work   1   2   3   4   5   Excellent
Paid attention to punctuation

Needs Work   1   2   3   4   5   Excellent
Sounded good

Total Words Read _____

Total Errors − _____

Correct WPM _____

71
Fiction

from **"Lost in the Land of Ishtaboli"**

by Don L. Birchfield

Follow McDaniel through a maze of air vents from which he can spy but cannot escape.

First Reading

	Words Read	Miscues

As soon as McDaniel was alone in his room, he went to the air | 14 | _____ |

vent beside his bed. Deftly, with the practiced hand of doing | 25 | _____

something for the third time, he removed the screws in the grille | 37 | _____

plate, hid them beneath his bed, placed the grille within easy | 48 | _____

reach of the air tube, wriggled into the tube feet first, on his | 61 | _____

stomach, reached out, picked up the grille, and fitted it snugly | 72 | _____

into place behind him. | 76 | _____

He wriggled backward up the small tube until it emptied into | 87 | _____

the familiar comfort of K42. This time, however, he moved | 97 | _____

quickly down K42 in the direction he had not taken on his two | 110 | _____

previous trips, thankful that K42 was large enough that he could | 121 | _____

move through it on his hands and knees. | 129 | _____

He had formulated a theory for the designation schemes of the | 140 | _____

air tubes, and if he was right he might find a way out of Ishtaboli. | 155 | _____

He passed up several small side tubes, confident that he was | 166 | _____

still in the area of the Academy of the Little Choctaws, but as he | 180 | _____

neared a large, arterial tube, where he would be able to walk | 192 | _____

upright, he crawled down a small side tube to get his bearings. | 204 | _____

Needs Work   1 2 3 4 5   Excellent
Paid attention to punctuation

Needs Work   1 2 3 4 5   Excellent
Sounded good

Total Words Read _____

Total Errors − _____

Correct WPM _____

71

Fiction

from "Lost in the Land of Ishtaboli"

by Don L. Birchfield

Follow McDaniel through a maze of air vents from which he can spy but cannot escape.

	Words Read	Miscues
As soon as McDaniel was alone in his room, he went to the air	14	_____
vent beside his bed. Deftly, with the practiced hand of doing	25	_____
something for the third time, he removed the screws in the grille	37	_____
plate, hid them beneath his bed, placed the grille within easy	48	_____
reach of the air tube, wriggled into the tube feet first, on his	61	_____
stomach, reached out, picked up the grille, and fitted it snugly	72	_____
into place behind him.	76	_____
He wriggled backward up the small tube until it emptied into	87	_____
the familiar comfort of K42. This time, however, he moved	97	_____
quickly down K42 in the direction he had not taken on his two	110	_____
previous trips, thankful that K42 was large enough that he could	121	_____
move through it on his hands and knees.	129	_____
He had formulated a theory for the designation schemes of the	140	_____
air tubes, and if he was right he might find a way out of Ishtaboli.	155	_____
He passed up several small side tubes, confident that he was	166	_____
still in the area of the Academy of the Little Choctaws, but as he	180	_____
neared a large, arterial tube, where he would be able to walk	192	_____
upright, he crawled down a small side tube to get his bearings.	204	_____

Needs Work   1   2   3   4   5   Excellent
Paid attention to punctuation

Needs Work   1   2   3   4   5   Excellent
Sounded good

Total Words Read   _____

Total Errors − _____

Correct WPM   _____

72

from *Terra Incognita:*
Travels in Antarctica
by Sara Wheeler

Note how the expedition experience remained in the minds
of two explorers.

First Reading

	Words Read	Miscues

∞∞∞

Fossil Bluff lies about 230 miles from Rothera on the east | 11 | _____
coast of Alexander Island. A group of men from the British | 22 | _____
Graham Land Expedition were the first to set foot there. They | 33 | _____
surveyed it roughly in 1936 and found Jurassic fossils, so they | 44 | _____
called it Fossil Camp. Lancelot Fleming, a member of the | 54 | _____
expedition who later became bishop of Norwich, made a film that | 65 | _____
was put on video 50 years later, with a narration by another | 77 | _____
member, the redoubtable Duncan Carse. Carse had gone on to | 87 | _____
become a successful actor, playing Dick Barton in a 1940s BBC | 98 | _____
radio series. His mellifluous voice perfectly captures the lost | 107 | _____
innocence of a golden age. After the expedition he spent some | 118 | _____
time alone [on] South Georgia [Island]. In a film about that he | 130 | _____
said, "I enjoyed a peace of mind there I've experienced nowhere | 141 | _____
else. It was an island where I belonged." In his diary he wrote of | 155 | _____
low clouds hanging in pearly streamers "like wraiths of the | 165 | _____
imagination. But through them and above, the unattainable | 173 | _____
heights of the Allardyce Range fired the skyline with stupendous | 183 | _____
beacons of icy luminosity . . . no one had ever seen them before: a | 195 | _____
thousand years might pass before they showed themselves again." | 204 | _____

Needs Work   1 2 3 4 5   Excellent
Paid attention to punctuation

Needs Work   1 2 3 4 5   Excellent
Sounded good

Total Words Read _____

Total Errors − _____

Correct WPM _____

from *Terra Incognita:*
Travels in Antarctica
by Sara Wheeler

Note how the expedition experience remained in the minds
of two explorers.

	Words Read	Miscues
Fossil Bluff lies about 230 miles from Rothera on the east	11	_____
coast of Alexander Island. A group of men from the British	22	_____
Graham Land Expedition were the first to set foot there. They	33	_____
surveyed it roughly in 1936 and found Jurassic fossils, so they	44	_____
called it Fossil Camp. Lancelot Fleming, a member of the	54	_____
expedition who later became bishop of Norwich, made a film that	65	_____
was put on video 50 years later, with a narration by another	77	_____
member, the redoubtable Duncan Carse. Carse had gone on to	87	_____
become a successful actor, playing Dick Barton in a 1940s BBC	98	_____
radio series. His mellifluous voice perfectly captures the lost	107	_____
innocence of a golden age. After the expedition he spent some	118	_____
time alone [on] South Georgia [Island]. In a film about that he	130	_____
said, "I enjoyed a peace of mind there I've experienced nowhere	141	_____
else. It was an island where I belonged." In his diary he wrote of	155	_____
low clouds hanging in pearly streamers "like wraiths of the	165	_____
imagination. But through them and above, the unattainable	173	_____
heights of the Allardyce Range fired the skyline with stupendous	183	_____
beacons of icy luminosity . . . no one had ever seen them before: a	195	_____
thousand years might pass before they showed themselves again."	204	_____

Needs Work 1 2 3 4 5 Excellent
Paid attention to punctuation

Needs Work 1 2 3 4 5 Excellent
Sounded good

Total Words Read _____

Total Errors – _____

Correct WPM _____

Progress Graph

1. For the first reading of the selection, put a red dot on the line above the selection number to show your correct words-per-minute rate.

2. For the second reading, put a blue dot on the line above the selection number to show your correct words-per-minute rate.

3. Make a graph to show your progress. Connect the red dots from selection to selection with red lines. Connect the blue dots with blue lines.

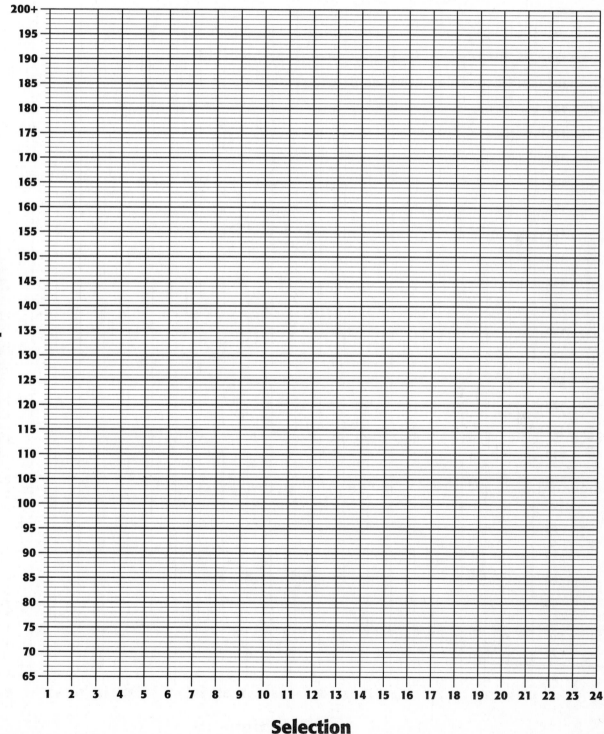

Selection

Progress Graph

1. For the first reading of the selection, put a red dot on the line above the selection number to show your correct words-per-minute rate.

2. For the second reading, put a blue dot on the line above the selection number to show your correct words-per-minute rate.

3. Make a graph to show your progress. Connect the red dots from selection to selection with red lines. Connect the blue dots with blue lines.

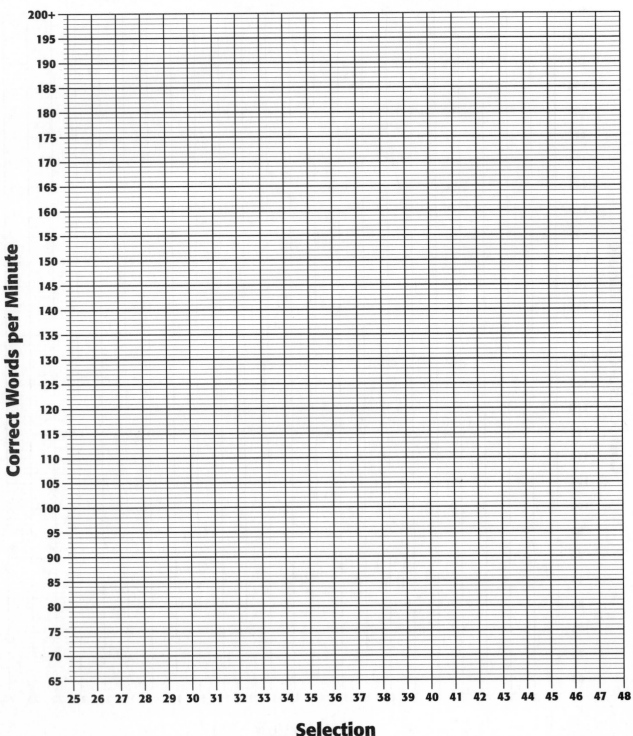

Correct Words per Minute

Selection

Progress Graph

1. For the first reading of the selection, put a red dot on the line above the selection number to show your correct words-per-minute rate.

2. For the second reading, put a blue dot on the line above the selection number to show your correct words-per-minute rate.

3. Make a graph to show your progress. Connect the red dots from selection to selection with red lines. Connect the blue dots with blue lines.

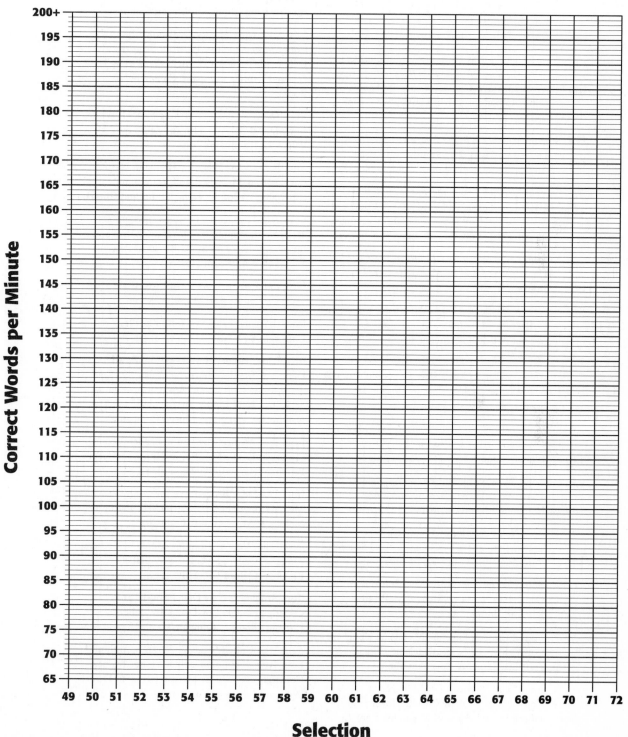

Correct Words per Minute

Selection

Acknowledgments